HOME

Nadia Fall

T0346703

National Theatre

OXFORD
UNIVERSITY PRESS

OXFORD
UNIVERSITY PRESS

Great Clarendon Street, Oxford, OX2 6DP, United Kingdom

Oxford University Press is a department of the University of Oxford. It furthers the University's objective of excellence in research, scholarship, and education by publishing worldwide. Oxford is a registered trade mark of Oxford University Press in the UK and in certain other countries

British Library Cataloguing in Publication Data
Data available

ISBN 978-0-19-842150-4

10 9 8 7 6 5

Printed and bound by CPI Group (UK) Ltd, Croydon, CR0 4YY

Acknowledgements
The publisher and author would like to thank the following for permission to use photographs and other copyright material:

Cover: Ellie Kurttz. All other photos © Ellie Kurttz, except: **p5:** © National Theatre; **p120:** Janine Wiedel Photolibrary/ Alamy Stock Photo; **p121:** UrbanImages/Alamy Stock Photo.

Every effort has been made to contact copyright holders of material reproduced in this book. Any omissions will be rectified in subsequent printings if notice is given to the publisher.

The publisher and National Theatre would like to thank Susie Ferguson and Jane Ball for writing and developing the activities.

The National Theatre would also like to thank the company of *Home*, whose names are listed in full on page 115.

Schools at the National Theatre:
The National Theatre opens up theatre for young people across the UK with inspiring creative projects, workshops and conferences for schools. To find out more visit: nationaltheatre.org.uk/secondary

Contents

Introduction

When you read on your own it is a very personal experience. You build a world in your imagination. You use the words of the writer to help you create a picture of what the people and setting look and sound like. Perhaps the writer tells you what a character is thinking or feeling, too. That world is yours – nobody else will ever be able to see it exactly as you do, even if they read the same novel themselves.

But with a play, the words on the page are just the starting point. They are not meant to simply be read and imagined – they are meant to be turned into a live performance. And although each of us will still have our own very personal idea of what the characters and the setting are like, taking a play from the script to the stage requires a group to imagine together. In a rehearsal room the actors and the director work together to bring the characters to life, to imagine what happened to them before the start of the play, and to explore what they are thinking and feeling. Before rehearsals start, the director and designers will begin to create the world of the play together starting with where the story happens and what the world of the play looks like. Even after this, the play isn't complete before an audience sees it, adding their collective imagination as well, to bring the story on stage alive.

The National Theatre is dedicated to making the very best theatre and sharing it with as many people as possible through: the theatres on the South Bank in London; touring and partnership productions; *NT Live* and *National Theatre: On Demand in Schools.*

At the National Theatre our rehearsal studios and workshops are constantly busy with actors, designers and directors working to bring plays to life – we produce around 25 each year. In a classroom you are studying a play, not making a production. But that doesn't mean you can't explore a play as actors, directors, designers and audience-members, thinking about the way you might approach a scene, or rehearsing different sections of the play to see how they change with different interpretations.

In this book you will find the text of the play that we produced at the National Theatre, together with images and resources which show you some of the ways the actors and production team worked to create our version of it. We hope this will inspire your own creative exploration of the play – which may be very different to ours. On the page, the play is just in one dimension. We hope you will enjoy bringing it to life.

Alice King-Farlow
Director of Learning
National Theatre

The play

Note on the play

Home is a piece of verbatim theatre. Verbatim means the repetition of words in the same way as they were originally spoken. This play has been created using real-life interviews, conversations and observations and therefore includes some expletives. Where these occur, a symbol '#!?&#!' has been inserted rather than the word being changed or replaced, in order to keep the intention and spirit of what is being said.

Character list

Singing Boy, a slight, mixed-race teenager
Young Mum, a young black woman
Bullet, a young black man
Tattoo Boy, a young white man with many tattoos on his arms and neck
Asian Young Mum, a British-Bengali teenager
Security Guard, a tall and imposing Nigerian man
Sharon, a white middle-aged East Londoner
Key Worker, a black middle-aged Londoner
Jade, a white teenager, only speaks in beats, six months pregnant
Eritrean Girl, a petite, recent refugee from Eritrea
Ex-Resident, a young black man with West Indian heritage
Garden Boy, a young white man, born and bred in East London
Young Mum's Sister, pregnant young black woman
Towelling Robe
Portugal, a black teenage girl
The Priest
EDF Person
Portugal's Boyfriend
Other Residents

Note
The residents and workers at Target East are all speaking to an
interviewer who, in performance, becomes the audience throughout.

Singing Boy

Act 1

*An anonymous inner-city high rise, London.
A **Young Woman** has her mobile phone to
her ear and is pushing a baby in a buggy back
and forth at the foot of the tower block. An
Older Woman is having a cigarette, shivering.
Two **Young Men** are milling about on the
concrete. At pressing a metal button you are
buzzed in through the main entrance door.
You notice the glass in the door is cracked and
that an argument has kicked off between the
boys outside. A poker-faced **Security Guard**
asks you who you are here to see.*

*The **Young Residents** are having breakfast.*

Scene 1 Singing Boy

*Enter **Singing Boy**. He sits.*

Singing Boy   My mum's house really… No, I consider my
place as a home as well, here as well…but still
feel a bit…maybe because I'm *new* I still feel
a bit…you know I don't, I still feel, I don't feel
this is my home *yet*. But as the months go by
and start getting my things together, I can call
it more of a home.

Well – *[Pause]* well – *[Smiling]* what led me to
living at Target is basically I got kicked out of
home when I was seventeen I didn't want to
go back. So they put me in a hostel and then
from there step by step, eventually step by
step…I was sent here, they 'referred' me here.

Um, no. Because I'm very to m…I keep myself
to myself. Because there are a lot of people in

this building and you don't even want to mess about with… There's people in this building that do drugs and all sorts. I'm a person who wants to keep *well*, well away from that. I keep my head down, because I don't want anyone to think I'm either giving them a dirty look or what I've seen in this building is that people get very – [Clicks fingers] aggravated so I want to avoid that and that's why I always mind my own business.

I've had problems with my mum for quite a while. And not just because of my mum, I mean Mum played parts obviously, but I'm not saying here that I was an angel because obviously I'm not…her boyfriend as well was getting involved but even before that, even before he came into the picture, there was already issues between us. But then that added on the tension, you know building up, and that made it so…whatever. But I remember the exact day that I left: it was the eighth of January at seven p.m. What I left, well I didn't leave, I got kicked out, and the police got involved but the police told me that, 'If your mum wants you to leave, then you have to leave'. But what they did not know, well they knew my age, but obviously they were ignorant to the fact, that even though I'm seventeen…she can't ask me to leave by law you still have to be with your mum.

Well my mum used to hit me before but not now. But shouting, swearing at me obviously.

And there was even a point my mum said to me, she said to me, 'I wish I aborted you.' [Pause]

And from that day on I said okay – *[Pause]* I'm going to stop trying to give a damn, I'm going to stop, trying to every time do things for people. Because I'm going to just do me.

What now? My days I wake up in the morning, I feel absolutely great. I get to do what I want, every moment I go to college. I sing I get do this it's part of my course. I sing, I dance, I act… I do everything. You want me to sing something now? Do you know Beyoncé? Yeah I'll sing that.

Singing Boy *sings* Halo *by Beyoncé.*

Thanks. Well what keeps me very motivated is the fact that every song I pick, every song I sing has to have meaning behind it and I feel that with every song I sing I'm here for a purpose, I'm here for a reason, to show the world…I was born. When I was at school, a all-boys school. I went to an all-boys school and it was not the easiest thing to get up on that stage and sing and not have people laugh at you. Or after you've finished your performance to say you're gay because you're singing or you're gay because you're singing a female song… And plus the way my voice sounds I felt every day I walked through those gates, I could have died.

The first time I fell in love, you can ask me that.

Silence.

I will tell you now… One thing, the only thing that I missed is that I have this one issue now in my sexuality…right now I don't know… where I'm going. I'm not sure what I like. I haven't told my family and I'm not planning to right now. Not at the moment I don't think… but that's one thing actually to tell you, I don't know. I'm…

I'm still struggling with that. But eventually I'll get to the bottom of it and hopefully soon.

My key workers the people who advise me, they're nice guys, if you stay here peacefully, keep your head down, like no warnings – nothing – you'll get your place one day – not straight away obviously but eventually. I respect everyone, I obey the rules, I do everything like – stay strong.

Scene 2 Breakfast club one

There is a breakfast table.

Music is playing on a mobile phone.

Young Mum   It's good you come breakfast club because you can interview everyone. Every Tuesday we do it. Umm…I know it's a bit cliché but everyone says you know, 'Home is where the heart is' and that's kinda what I think as well, wherever you're comfortable, you feel like you know that you can relax and you don't have to worry or anything that's what I think home is.

Bullet   Home would be the land we come from really and truly it wouldn't be where we are today.

Song: *Keys*

[Singing] I bet it feels warmer with them
Warmer with them in your hands
I bet you feel stronger with them
Pinky finger spin it man.

Tattoo Boy   Home. Is er…it's whatever you make it really.

Whatever you make like, your surroundings, wherever you feel comfortable to lay your head or sometimes wherever you do have to lay your head.

Singing Boy   My mum's house really… I don't feel this is my home yet.

Asian Young Mum   To me home is a place where you're feeling safe, feeling happy… Or just becomes a house if you not happy where you are…it's just…a house.

Security Guard   Yes. Well I would say, personally, I would say Target is my home because I spend the majority of my time here.

Young Mum

Bullet [Singing] I feel there's no place like it
That it's warm when you feel it on both sides
They say you can't live without it
So what does that mean for my life?

Sharon Home is the most important place…for anybody and, for me, it's a place for, to relax, it's the safest and most securest place as far as I'm concerned that what you should be and it's about family and…and enjoying that time at…home.

Residents [Singing] I'm longing for those keys
Oh how I'm longing for those keys
Somewhere I can call my home
My home
Call the home
My home
Somewhere I can call my home
My home
Call the home
My home
Oh how I'm longing for those.

*The **Residents** tell us all at once what home means to them.*

I'll find my way home
My way home
My way home

Bullet Oh how I'm longing for those keys.

*The **Residents** leave the space.*

*__Sharon__ and **Asian Young Mum** are left at the table.*

Sharon Your hair looks nice.

Asian Young Mum Yeah I had it done yesterday…

Sharon	Well it suits ya. I tell you I need mine done. Did you do it across the road?
Asian Young Mum	Nah, I went to one of them photo-shoot things, where they do your hair and make-up for free and that. Take photos.
Sharon	*[Playing with baby]* Ah did you get your photos done with this angel? I'd like to see them…
Asian Young Mum	Nah, I don't think I'm getting them, they were asking loads for 'em.
Sharon	Oh yeah they charge loads. What you up to today then?
Asian Young Mum	I'm doing the interview thing a bit later so I'll just wait here for a bit… *[Addressing the interviewer]* No it's fine. I don't mind waiting.
Sharon	Right then, shall we go in there?

Scene 3 Sharon's office

Sharon	Okay? Right. I work at Target East which is a foyer for two hundred and ten young people in East London, erm…and the young people who live here are provided with accommodation and at the same time we look at their personal needs, their support needs, erm…education, training, so, it's a very whole-istic erm…view… erm…it's very holistic so we look at all their needs erm…and we take young people for up to two years.
	I was a single mother for quite a while but, so, I didn't work for quite a while when my children were growing up and then I decided to, that I wanted to do something but I always had a, to be quite honest, my interest was

always with working with offenders that was wh…what really, what I really enjoyed doing for some reason I'm not quite sure why…erm…but, so when my children went to junior school that's when I went to university and I studied psycho-social, and erm…part of psycho-social was around erm, criminology and stuff like that, so I did that for three years and in my last year I did a year's voluntary work with the probation service, so, and I really enjoyed that but what I didn't enjoy was, you was getting to meet all these young people who were going through the system but you never got to see any outcomes because…people were coming in, you'd sign them up or you might you might take them to rehab, you might take young people out on reparation orders you go with them, make sure they do it and get involved with them and…but you never saw them after that so you don't know whether they was successful…but with here what I liked erm…but what I liked about what I saw was…you worked with them throughout that whole period so you knew whether you'd made a difference to…to the young person's life so, yeah, more satisfaction and I guess, in a way a little bit more personal as well you know, because you know, you have to take into account professional boundaries, et cetera et cetera, but you do feel, there is no doubt that you have to have a connection with a young person, you get to know the young person, you get to know what makes them tick and you get to like them and you want them to succeed.

Key Worker walks in.

Key Worker	Yeah, are we still going to the afternoon meeting?
Sharon	This is one of our key workers. Yeah definitely yeah – oh could you do the printouts? Oh no don't worry I'll do 'em.
Key Worker	You sure?
Sharon	Yeah, yeah.
Key Worker	Okay.

Key Worker walks out.

Sharon	Well there was lots of problems going on here and they thought it would be a challenge for me to basically deal with the antisocial behaviour. There was young people who didn't want to get referred here, there was people scared to come out of their flats. It had a terrible name you know, no matter who you spoke to…in…whoever in the community, Target East was, was labelled as, like…you know…this run-down place full of gangs, erm you know, and it wasn't a place you'd wanna live. So when they asked me to come over here I didn't want to come you know, even I didn't you know, even me! But I was told I had to come basically and I did come and there were lots of issues you know it was sad really because it is a young person's home and you don't want anybody to feel scared to come out of their flat. The police had a terrible perception of the residents here and of the staff they felt that staffs were colluding with the residents. The relationship between police and staff was…you know at a breaking point…you know there was no…they…police didn't trust the staff, staff didn't trust the

police, it was really bad. So there was a lot of work to do, residents had no respect for staff. I was quite shocked when I first came here they weren't following rules but then they weren't getting picked up on it. Drug dealers were blatantly coming in the building and saying 'I'm doing my ting' they just didn't care, they'd just tell ya. So yeah there was a lot of work to do around it. It was very challenging at the time.

There was visitors coming to the building that were, oh it was horrendous how they abused the residents and staff so we took out injunctions which was a first for Target East, in three or four months we took out like twelve injunctions and they were excellent because they came with a committal to prison so if they breached they would get taken to court. I used to have arguments on front desk with some of them and they used to say to me, 'I dare you, call the police and see what happens' and you can't back down and I just had to pick the phone up in front of them, 999, and the message got out.

So it paid off big time really…

Singing Boy walks in.

Singing Boy	Oh sorry.
Sharon	No you're alright.
Singing Boy	I got the letter through.
Sharon	Which one?
Singing Boy	The housing one. About my bond scheme.
Sharon	Oh.

Singing Boy Shall I come back?

Sharon No I'll have a look now. Just one sec.

Singing Boy Oh, thanks.

Singing Boy exits.

Sharon I don't think you can switch off when you have a job like this, I have had hundreds of sleepless nights. It's a pain in the arse to be quite honest. I am a thinker anyway, so, you know, it's difficult you go a bed you're tired, you've had long days and you don't sleep half the night because all you're thinking about is what you're gonna do the next day to resolve this, do this, do this. Anyway, what are you going to do?

Sharon shows the interviewer out to the office foyer area.

Young Mum Oh so I can take you on a tour now if you like? We can start with the mother-and-baby section – Oh, do you want me to go get him? Cos I could – okay, I'll go get him just wait here I'll be five minutes.

Scene 4 New resident

Jade is in the breakfast room, on the phone to the council. All of her lines are spoken in beatbox.

Eritrean Girl is overheard through an office door that is ajar.

Jade [Beatboxes] Hi, yeah, I wanted to talk to someone about my housing benefit.

Jade is put on hold.

[Beatboxes] Hi, I wanted to talk to someone about my housing benefit.

[Beatboxes] Oh –

Jade *is put on hold.*

[Beatboxes] Hi, I wanted to talk to someone about my housing benefit.

Jade *is put on hold.*

[Beatboxes] #!?&#! sake.

[Beatboxes] Yeah, I've literally been put on hold three times.

[Beatboxes] My name?

[Beatboxes] Jade Simmonds.

[Beatboxes] Please don't put me on hold.

[Beatboxes, frustrated] Okay.

Jade *is put on hold.*

Jade

[Beatboxes] I'm trying to get through to someone about my housing benefit form.

[Beatboxes] This is the fourth time I've been put on hold.

Jade is put on hold.

[Beatboxes] If I don't get through to someone, I won't be able to pay my rent.

[Beatboxes] Not a funny situation.

[Beatboxes] I'm at Target East.

[Beatboxes] I'm six months pregnant.

[Beatboxes] You're punching me for it.

[Beatboxes] Can I be put through to your manager?

[Beatboxes] I'm organised about these things.

[Beatboxes] I need the money.

Jade is put on hold.

She hangs up.

She throws her phone.

Her baby kicks, she soothes it and leaves.

Key Worker	Why did you need to leave?
Eritrean Girl	My house was burgled…and when I put my key inside my door…is open but I know my mind is open – but I shook and I'm trying to open it and I tried, oh my God, it's open. When I open my door…everything is mess and…oh my God…
Key Worker	They took everything?
Eritrean Girl	They literally took, even they took…DVD and something like, very easy things maybe they want money, I don't have money they put

	every, my clothes over floor and…er…the dirty, the clean one, everything is mess…the house is…
Key Worker	Right so did you tell the landlord?
Eritrean Girl	Yes and I was very shocked and I call for landlord and the landlord 'Can you come please?' because I was very shaking…um… and I don't know this new, just only one year…I don't know the life or how is here but at that moment, I became homeless.
Key Worker	So you left that place?
Eritrean Girl	I left that place because of the…I ask them the landlord to…fix my door… They knows already my house is burgled they say 'Why you call us? Call to police.'
Key Worker	So they didn't attend?… They didn't fix the door?
Eritrean Girl	No. She say you now just call for police, he can help you what you want. Okay. I agree and call for police. Police come, say they don't find anything, so…at the end they ask me to fix the door, the police. How much? – A hundred pound…oh my God, I don't have hundred pound. I don't have anyone here, to go even and to sleep with and…the police left, they said okay, and they told me to put the, my chair on the door…
Key Worker	So how long have you been homeless?
Eritrean Girl	Um…month and half I think…
Key Worker	Where have you been living?
Eritrean Girl	Church friends already one year I spend with

	them and I have the friends and I went to, today your home, tomorrow another…
Key Worker	So you were homeless for a month and a half?
Eritrean Girl	Homeless yeah. Homeless month and half and I…was very, that one month, like a one year for me. When you go some people they don't want to have you because they have another thing to do in their home and I feel even when I call I feel shame – what can I do? But I don't have choice.
Key Worker	Do you have contact with your family?
Eritrean Girl	Contract?
Key Worker	No, family – you have family?
Eritrean Girl	No, no, not here no – sorry my English very, even now I can't explain what I want to tell you!
Key Worker	Children?
Eritrean Girl	One daughter…
Key Worker	She is living…
Eritrean Girl	[Avoiding eye contact] …In my home country…
Key Worker	I'll get you the forms just a second.

Key Worker exits office.

Young Mum returns to the office foyer area with *Ex-Resident*.

Scene 5 The tour begins

Young Mum Sorry about that, *[Pointing at **Ex-Resident**]* this one was taking ages. This is part of the mother-and-baby unit so everyone lives in these flats down here…so yeah, all along these flats are the ground floor, this is called the mother-and-baby unit, every single person in these flats down here, has a child, or is pregnant. Yeah.

EDF Person walks past.

The lady, she's from EDF, that's the EDF lady, basically she's probably come to check somebody's meters or something.

Ex-Resident What flat you looking for? Twenty-three?

Asian Young Mum walks past.

She checks the meter case anyone has wired it or… Yeah there's a lot of, like, fraud! Serious!

Young Mum Yeah yeah yeah, so, there's this guy that comes in the block yeah, you give him £20 and he puts a £50 electric on your thing yeah – but! – if you get clocked, I know someone who did it and then British Gas clocked on and they take money out of her.

The tour moves outside to the courtyard at Target.

Garden Boy is in the courtyard.

Now here, this is the garden, this is all mother-and-baby unit all bottom-floor flats are mother-and-baby unit like I said… Are you alright with him? He gets really heavy after a while I tell you!

Ex-Resident	People ask me, what are you doing back here? And I always say to them, you know, I'm not just here for me but for others, we're doing, I've started this garden project and…getting lot of fruit, strawberries.
	Yeah, I've been here six years, and I've lived here for three, cos I was staying, I was staying at a mate's, like here basically, cos I was homeless, I started homeless…we're still going in circles.
Young Mum	Carrots and stuff yeah, there was tomatoes, there was like strawberries and that.
Ex-Resident	Yeah there's potatoes as well, if you…
Young Mum	Yeah the strawberries I'm not gonna lie, we ate them.
Ex-Resident	That in the middle, it's for mothers and babies, got toys in it – but I think it's closed right now.
Young Mum	Um, it's not closed – I think there was a heater but it wasn't working but the fact is because it's greenhouse it's either really, really cold or really, really warm so…and the weather's been lately, really cold yeah.
	They move the tour back inside. **Garden Boy** *approaches with a garden trowel.*
Garden Boy	I've been here nearly two years…and it's been struggling, struggling living here, it's just hard. Uh, well me and my mum, my mum had my little brother when I was sixteen…and then all my mum did was say, make him a drink, make your brother food, do this, do that, do this, I literally had no time to myself, except for night-time and then obviously I was awake all the way through the night, tired during the day and I had to do more stuff and it led – it

led to depression and anxiety… I didn't even go school because I used to basically just had to do so much for my mum, plus I was bullied at school so that didn't help either. Mum didn't care. And then…one day I snapped, and, had a go at my mum and then she wanted me to leave so I left… I was on the streets for about a month…or so, I used to sleep in the park up the road on the benches, then I eventually had the courage to tell my girlfriend. I lived with her for a couple of months…then I went First Point, and then…I ended up here.

A home? A place where I feel safe…walk in, cos like here, I walk in, I literally, put the latch on…the chain, and the bottom lock…and then I put a towel at the bottom?… And I think that's quite sad that I don't feel safe even though there's security, two electric doors and then my door.

The people that live here to be exact, just, you walk around and you see like, there's a guy called Blunt who I know, lives a few doors away from me, I'm not sure if I should be saying this but…

He's umm he said to me that um, he was caught for burglary and I'm like, okay, this guy lives three doors down from me and he's been done for burglary, there's drug dealers in the building…it just doesn't feel like a safe environment, cos when I first moved in here, I think it was about two months after moving in here some guy got stabbed in the neck.

In this, in the building yeah.

Garden Boy

I don't know if fatally, I know he got stabbed in the neck.

I feel more safer out there than I do in here.

The tour continues.

Ex-Resident And the next thing we're looking to do is add a bit of colours to these walls.

Young Mum No they're not.

Ex-Resident And just…

Young Mum Don't lie.

Ex-Resident	Listen, I'm giving my view young lady.
Young Mum	You can't change it. We're not allowed.

Baby cries.

Oh I'll take him. I think he needs a change. Go get me a nappy from my sister—

Ex-Resident	What?
Young Mum	Please just do it. Can you just wait for us in the reception bit yeah? I won't be long…

Asian Young Mum is seen up on another floor.

Young Mum and *Ex-Resident* leave the interviewer alone. An office door is ajar and the conversation overheard between *Key Worker* and *Bullet*.

Scene 6 Dressing down

Key Worker	Right you're in arrears of three grand. What? Did you hear me?

Bullet is silent.

You've not been paying what you're supposed to, you've not responded to any letters either…

Bullet	I haven't got no letters…
Key Worker	So you haven't got no letters from East Thames? Well I know for a fact security have been putting letters under your door and I've personally been posting letters to your door. So that's pure nonsense!
Bullet	Yeah…

Key Worker	What? Stop mumbling. That's not going to help you now. Do you realise you're going to be evicted? Do you?

Bullet is silent.

If you get evicted have you got somewhere to go?

Bullet	*No.*
Key Worker	No.
Bullet	Nah man…
Key Worker	No mumbling. Sit up man. This isn't a joke. You can't come in here looking at the floor without your #!?&#! together. You've got to wake up. This is serious. Do you think I'm being too hard on you?

Bullet is silent.

[Picking up the phone] Hi I'm a key worker for a young man who's under threat of eviction from our foyer. Yeah I'll hold. *[To Bullet]* You've got to ask yourself what can I do to turn my life around. How can you organise yourself. Start opening those letters, stop burying your head in the sand. The only one that can help you right now is you.

Key Worker exits office and notices interviewer.

Are you waiting for someone? Interviews? No I didn't hear – have you cleared it with Sharon? Right.

Key Worker exits, leaving Bullet in the office.

Scene 7 Babies and boyfriends

Young Mum in the corridor. *Asian Young Mum* in her flat.

Young Mum	Yeah if you're not mother and baby you don't normally stay here cos the lift is rubbish, and the stairs bringing the baby up is too much for them but the higher you are up, the quicker you're gonna get out the flat if you're pregnant cos it's a risk for you…
Asian Young Mum	I'm on the seventh floor. And the lifts as well, the lifts keep breaking down and going up and down them stairs and.
Young Mum	My son is nine months old.
Asian Young Mum	My daughter is nine months.
Young Mum	Oh it's great. It's like um…I dunno, you can't explain being a mother to someone who's not, if they are a mother then they'll automatically understand. But um…it's, it's just…I dunno at first you're scared and that, when you're pregnant, you're oh am I gonna be enough am I gonna do enough? Am I gonna get everything I need to get for him? But then…it's just pure determination and cos you know you know this is your son, no one else is gonna look after him but you…so…yeah I just…uh it's been great.
Asian Young Mum	After I had her I think that was my, my main breakthrough for me personally that is when I put my foot down and I said you know what, I'm not letting her go through this. Yeah it gave me a reason to…wake up, every day.
Young Mum	I love him now and it's weird…to know like… now that you're a mum, you can't imagine not being a mum.

Asian Young Mum	Cos my room and my living room is together we're trapped in one room so she's so used to having me in one place, cos I've got nowhere to go like I have to place her in bed and I have to make sure I turn off the TV cos she's a light sleeper as well so I don't have time to myself cos the room and the living room's together and where do I go, kitchen? Do what exactly? Apart from cook, I can't sit in the kitchen.

So when she sleeps I do nothing I sit there, if I can't sleep I will just sit there.

Yeah it will take about seven to fourteen years to get your own permanent place. Yeah – you have to bid for seven to fourteen years. But you can be put into private housing so it's not your home but it's a house.

Young Mum	It didn't feel like a burden to me because I'd already prepared myself like, I know I'm not gonna sleep for like months…but then he started sleeping much earlier than I thought, he's a good boy yeah, I was alright, I was lucky.
Asian Young Mum	So well what happened, I went Bangladesh for a year and eight months cos of my father, um, so I missed Year 11, I come back and to them it's like my father, it's never enough, no matter how good you are it's like, you gotta do more, you gotta cover more wanted to go out – I couldn't, but because I wanted to – I'm so bad in his eyes.

Then well it was, I was on a day out, I was telling my parents I'm going work – *[Laughs]* and…got on the bus, met the father…on the bus…what a crazy meeting…and he was already drunk and we just got talking and we just clicked and to me that lifestyle it was just like – wow! You're drinking you're having fun – and I didn't have groups of friends that used to go out and drink cos I wasn't allowed out and the work lot is just – at work. So that was the first time I met someone, who's…you know doing their own thing, it was just like wow to me then he was like yeah, try a bit, tried it, loved the drink. *[Laughs]*

I never been West End until I met him, took me there and it was just a new life to me and it was like…woah…so, we just went out and just seen the lights and everything… *[Laughs]*

Yeah I was madly in love with him and to me it was, learning everything from him and having fun and I just wanted to be with him, I used to go and see him in prison um…obviously my parents didn't know anything about him in prison but…

Young Mum sings the first two lines of Sweet Nothing by Calvin Harris featuring Florence Welch.

Young Mum   It's funny cos I met him on the bus and um… and then I saw him in college and I was like 'Oh hi!' and – *[Laughs]* we've been together about four years now. He's been around much more than I expected like, he's really good with him.

Young Mum and Asian Young Mum sing the next two lines of Sweet Nothing by Calvin Harris featuring Florence Welch.

Asian Young Mum   There was a few issues um, domestic violence and stuff like that which got a bit out of hand… I think there was an incident outside where he did hit me in a DLR station and then he headbutted me and stuff and the police got involved and, this has happened several times before but I just never put a statement through and then at the time I just thought enough's enough…

Young Mum and *Asian Young Mum* *continue to sing.*

His family didn't even call when she was born, they haven't asked how she was… I went through hell when I was living with his family, it was just me a slave there to be honest, just cook for fourteen people…

I used to wake up in the morning and I just used to look at an empty mirror basically, I just used to see through me like, I didn't feel as if I existed sometimes…you're in the house, you just can't see yourself, you just, you just feel as if that's your life and…it's gonna end there.

I was on depression tablets as well, the first miscarriage I had was due to domestic violence so to me it was, I felt as though something was taken from me so I always wanted a baby since.

I do allow him to come here yeah, but I will have to, because of her, that's one good thing about Target though…which is extremely good for me and especially security…umm…but he does come down, if he does come down, if I know he's drunk I wouldn't let him near me.

Scene 8 Bullet

Bullet is chased by a masked gunman. He relives the time he was shot.

Bullet Jail, it's like a withdrawal. So you know when you are locked up. Everything is taken away from you, you know. So your withdrawals kick in. Then your thoughts about your family and all that stuff on top of it, like in bed. I was in bed sleeping one time I'm hot but I'm cold at the same time but I'm sweating too and I was like, this is the weirdest thing ever. It was like the longest night of my life ever. It was it was the longest night ever.

After jail, I got shot outside my house on the doorstep. Man got shot outside my house my mum was all running out with her shoes off everything – crazy.

I knew it went in but I knew it wasn't in, do you know what I am trying to say cos I was still able to move apart from blood so it's just when your life flashes before you makes you, like, you can literally see everything in the space of three seconds and you are thinking about your family and that but you are still trying to find your route and get away at the same time. It's like triple-tasking in your head. It's crazy. I got away from him. He was still shooting after me. I was lucky really. Cos I was point-blank around the vehicle he's just aiming at me. Your eyes, when your eyes intertwine with someone else's, they lock and you know that person. He set out with an agenda, it was to kill not to hit to injure it was proper murder he wanted to do. His persistence told me he did want to murder me cos he let off like four shots so it weren't just like, it weren't just like he came to have fun. It was broad day, it was like two p.m. it wasn't night-time so like.

Song: *Bullets*

[Singing] Something you don't Ever want to Happen to you
you don't Ever want to Happen to you
bein' Shot's not Fun man
What ever PredicamenT you're in
dunnoO, I used to Think i was inVincible
inniT, so when i Got shot, it Changed me inniT, made me
Feel… dunnoO, I'm a Victim
inniT, different From bein' a Suspect inniT, then you
Think, rhass, today I Really could've Passed, as you
Bleed fast, But adrenaLine hides diSasters, and
Time paSSes like the Bullets from 'em #!?&#!,
#!?&#! put a Bullet through my Rass
#!?&#! put a Bullet through my Rass
imagine If that same Bullet hit my Marge
I could Cuss the same Me from the Past
bowlin' Past in my Superhuman Stance, like.

Bullet sings Ghetto Story *by Cham.*

It's just that it's hard the way of life is just weird for me I don't know I just think that life's not fair innit. Sometimes I just wish it's better that we weren't here, or better that I weren't here. Cos then I wouldn't have problems to deal with.

Bullet exits.

Bullet

Scene 9 The tour continues

Young Mum	If we go that way and then we go up.
Ex-Resident	No but still we'll have to go all round…
Young Mum	No you don't have to go round why do you have to go round?
Ex-Resident	Listen, I've been in the block for the last six years, she doesn't know the building.

Young Mum	Shut up. This is my place yeah –

The front desk yeah, when you come here um, you need to have a resident to sign you in, you need a photo ID with your name and a clear picture, or else our lovely security guard's not gonna sign you in, it's fact, that's the rules um…most visitors in the block you have to be here after two to get signed in but basically because I'm Chairman of this place I kind of went out of my way to make sure that they could have a little bit earlier for the mother and baby because we do need that bit of extra support, especially when you've just had a child, it's really hard and if people do wanna come and see you two o'clock is too late…for them to come see you.

Sharon walks by.

Residents start to arrive at the front desk.

Ex-Resident	You put your fob through and you look hard through there and you speak to a Mr Stephenson.
Young Mum	Yeah one of the most popular faces that you can see at our reception.

It's much better now, inside the foyer, our security here, with Stephenson yeah, unless you're some kind of magician I don't think you're getting past him to get in here…yeah… apart from residents letting idiots in, it's alright yeah…

*The **Security Guard** doesn't look impressed.*

They go off on the tour.

Scene 10 Security

Security Guard in his booth at reception.

Security Guard This week I been doing seven to three and then tomorrow I'll be doing three to nine and then two days after I'm gonna be doing nights so you can see that from Monday to Sunday I'm in.

Yeah um, a lot could go wrong at any point in time, why because most residents um… they get frustrated with their issues. We try to ask them what's the problem, they just get frustrated and…lose it so all we do is try to calm them down.

I would say night shift is calmer on the ground than it's within a week.

The Security Guard looks at some mugshot pictures on the wall.

These are nice faces you know, but um, yeah as you can see I would tell you that all of them are visitors, no resident yeah, that is an example of people who are coming here to make trouble to like, no obey the rules of signing in and all that and we also stopped them from coming in here because sometimes they say they are coming for a visit and they spend the night here which is not right you know, and they are very, very violent, being abusive.

Um, yeah actually, a lot changed because we really did work so hard, you know then I used to do night, I was just on night. They tend to come over here, you know to meet their friends, smoke, they try to, you know destroy the properties you know playing with the fire –

ha ha you know.

Kicking the female doors open and all kind of stuff, you know molestation was actually going on so we had to really get into the building at that time, really I was like…behind everyone but good thing I was a good guy, really calmed them down as much as I can, so the majority of them had the confidence in me that if I'm around things will definitely work out well you know so.

*The **Security Guard** pauses to deal with some **Residents**.*

Security Guard

There was one resident who was sadly killed nearby.

…He used to be a quiet one, you know I have been working here for quite some time, I never seen him in any argument form with no one he just a friend of everyone, you know, but and that one fateful day—

Sharon walks by and meets Eritrean Girl at reception. The Security Guard goes to join them.

Sharon You looking for a mouse?

Yeah come through I've got to get me potatoes out the oven.

Sharon leads the interviewer into the breakfast room and attends to the oven.

Scene 11 Refugee

Eritrean Girl is pursued by some male residents who are coming on to her, she seems uncomfortable with their presence.

Eritrean Girl Can we go to the office? Thanks.

Eritrean Girl and interviewer find an empty office.

Er…because you know our country Eritrea.

There is, religion, because of my religion it's not possible to um…to be free and to worship in Jesus Christ so because of that I…came out from that place.

The government rule the country but this is about the religion our religion is different. If you maybe they found you when you worship on a place, they gonna come, the police come and took you to prison.

Umm…2008. I left that country. From my country to Yemen from Yemen to France by plane and half of by boat. From France to here I came by, you know by lorry? You know lorry? They brought us to… lorry and we get in, eight people together.

Um…you know the France one is very hard, because you know the…the agent brought me to one of, some people he introduced me to them and this is your country people and you have to look after her and to bring her and they said…okay and four, three boys and…three boys and I, the man is, he left he gave me money, like, to eat and to…get the hotel for one night and…um…when we going together with those boys, two of them very I scared of them because they flirting, something to have me you know…to do…the one is okay…he doesn't show anything he's thinking about future and – oh my God…I'm gonna spend tonight…with who…with which one? And…I don't know them just he left me with someone and…they are my country people but I don't know…even they are boys…if they are girls I don't mind and when we go to hotel, they have two rooms and we are four: me and three others…

So…I was thinking to have my only…but how? Is not possible to sleep for three, they say two, two. Okay… *[Pause]* I got on my knees and I pray, which one is good man…that doesn't touch me… I just sit down and I think about all of them…and suddenly I feel…I feel

Eritrean Girl

one, something this good and…we pay the hotel yeah? I said to them, 'I'm gonna choose to sleep with one. Him.' They said, 'Okay, okay why don't you choose me? Why don't you choose us? Whhhy? Nnno! We don't leave him just to you?' And then one of them he lay down on the bed and said, 'Okay, I'm sleeping here. Come sleep.' I said, 'Can you go out please? Already I paid for this room.' I say, 'Can you please go to your room, you two go?' They say, 'Oh my God how do you know he's very good man?' Because they know him, he is their friend. How, how is she know he's good man? How?! They wondering but I feel inside…

Inside the lorry there is a place, you know, they know they put us something in something, and we sit down when the policeman come and when they…looking, they don't find and the car is passed.

Song: *O Lord*

[Singing] O, my feet, where have you taken me?
It is dark, it is dark
and I can't see the light
No, I can't see the light
O Lord,
are you walking with me?
O Lord,
are you walking with me?
O Lord,
are you walking with me?
O Lord,
are you walking with me?

The car is leave us one place, even we don't know this is London just, we me and one man, the guy who was in the car.

The car is leave us one place and we walking to another. We don't know anywhere.
We don't know anywhere, we don't have anything.

Just we walking yeah.

[Singing] O, my feet, where have you taken me?
It is dark, it is dark
and I can't see the light
No, I can't see the light
O Lord,
are you walking with me?
O Lord,
are you walking with me?
O Lord,
are you walking with me?
O Lord,
are you walking with me?

Suddenly like miracle you know I found him I found one guy on the street Somalian guy. We know the Somalia face. So straight away when I see him, this is Somalia I have to go and ask him.

He was helpful man. He brought me, 'Okay come come come' and he brought me to go that is the office you can go tell them everything. We explain everything we get somewhere to stay that night everything.

Yeah that's miracle for me like miracle, how do you believe that?

Scene 12 This is England

Tattoo Boy enters the common breakfast space.

Tattoo Boy   Umm...going round seeing all my friends and that, like there was one of my friends

who lived in this block but he passed away
unfortunately last year and that, but the last
Christmas we had we'd meet up with each
other, him come down with a cup of tea and
that, I'd have a cup of tea, we smoke a puff
each and that, chill out, talk and that and then
probably go like, say see you later to each
other…go round see our other friends and
then go see our family, our mums and that…
say, 'Merry Christmas' and whatnot to them,
then probably just go round to our other
mates' and then just chill with them, have
a good time, have a laugh and that, come
back to the block, meet up, have a little party,
something like that yeah. Yeah…he was a
resident here.

Sharon   We lost our resident Daniel, over at Westfield.

Tattoo Boy   It was at Westfield like, the only person who's
been killed at Westfield.

Sharon   I erm…received a phone call from staff who
said that one of the residents had come
back here…and said something had been
happening in Westfield…and a stabbing had
taken place and they believed it was Daniel
and…would I find…was…you know some of
the residents were a bit upset.

Tattoo Boy   The way it happened and there's loads of
different stories like. Just some #!?&#! walking
about with a knife and that d'you know what
I mean why would you go to a shop with a
knife? D'you know what I mean why would
you do that for? Obviously going out looking
to hurt someone but people don't think and
that cos they're so immature, young-minded

Tattoo Boy

and they get…like basically fed a pack of lies by older lot of people who tell them to go make a name for theirself and that you know, stuff like that it's just…stupidness.

Sharon Two policeman turned up and were standing outside his room so it was very obvious that it, you know, something had happened…erm… so that's how I found out you know…

Tattoo Boy He was a good man.

Sharon He was a very good resident. He was very well liked.

Tattoo Boy Daniel was a good guy man he always told me as well, the biggest, like #!?&#! wimp can kill the biggest man as well like. And it seemed like that was true man, cos he was a good guy…and all that, d'you know what I mean… he was a really decent friend.

Sharon He was very well liked.

Tattoo Boy Yeah, yeah he had quite a big impact on everyone…he was proper loving, bubbly guy and that, friendly…he was a cushty geezer, they got memorials put up for him we had a fundraising week for him and everything so it's alright…

Sharon We did a week of events for Daniel erm…so we held a barbecue, invited all the families, friends, held it outside erm…we did some fundraising so we could help, you know when that happened it was a real turning point for the staff and the residents, I think we got to know each other and we supported each other a lot better, and what came out of that was that the residents…actually, said that they missed community events where people could get to know each other and that sort of made a lot, it had an impact on a lot of people, people met each other for the first time… you know. It's amazing that this building is so diverse…erm…and…you know, I've seen, they mix so well a lot of the residents you know, erm, and I've seen a lot of respect amongst, you know, a lot of the young people whether, it don't matter where you're from, you know.

Tattoo Boy It's the culture. It's the culture of the area, it's the…it's…people…I dunno, just making up their own rules yeah d'you know what I mean, just thinking they can do I dunno, it's just the culture, the culture the life in London and that, d'you know what I mean? It's just the way it is.

Round this area, I ain't racist or anything but this is mainly like, a black person's area, where I'm white and I don't dress with all the #!?&#! tracksuits and trousers past my #!?&#! and that, I don't get pulled over d'you know what I mean? Yeah. Cos the black people stereotype theirself anyway, so, they've only got theirself to blame. They say 'We're the minority,' but did you read on the news yesterday, the majority are now the minority.

In London, all together, white people are the minority. White, English people are minority.

Africans are the majority and then Caribbeans then Asians.

Because you see um…Polish shops, Jamaican shops, dadadada, but then if you see like an English shop or something, someone will blatantly come out with, 'Oh that's racist.' You know that you know how it works cos for instance you go to Poland, you go to China, you go to India…you'll never see a, a church of England there or anything, you'll never see a shop saying, 'Oh, only English shop,' and that, I'm not saying that only English people or Polish shops that are here only Polish people are allowed in them but they don't have just like, an English shop will have food for every other country that's why you don't even really need to leave London to travel the world and that, you see it all, it's multicultural, but, the problem is, it's out of control now d'you know what I mean like you…

Nowadays, you have to keep your own…you have to keep the history of the country going d'you know what I mean? Within a hundred years' time this country won't even have history d'you know what I mean if you think from all over the world it'll be there won't be one English person, I don't reckon, in about a hundred years. They'll all have some other different ethnic minority or background. Like you know I'm saying, no matter, everyone who's come to this country, yeah, like all different foreign people you go back to any one of them foreign countries and I guarantee you they still have their native people there sort of thing you know what I mean?

My girlfriend's not English, she's Turkish. Doesn't bother me. *[Pause]* Doesn't bother me at all but I'm just saying enough's enough like because for instance, if you go to them other countries you won't see none of our #!?&#! in their country and even in, even though this is England you'll never see English stuff in this country d'you understand what I'm saying. Like I went Wilkinson the other day and the only flags they sell are Pakistani and Nigeria. In the English shop, Wilkinson and where the #!?&#! is the English flag then…oh yeah and Polish flag they sold, I'm like, just because they're white don't mean they're English d'you know what I mean, they're #!?&#! Polish man.

And like everyone who's not English like, they're just rinsing the country, bleeding it dry and when someone English just tries bleeding the country dry cos they're actually suffering because all these foreigners are bleeding their country dry, they get in trouble and they get #!?&#! right up.

Young Mum enters.

Young Mum   Alright? You alright babe? I'll come back.

Tattoo Boy   England just gets the #!?&#! taken out of it d'you know what I mean? That's all it is it's a #!?&#!-takers' country. Bunch of mugs like.

Song: *No Shoulder to Cry On*

Security Guard   *[Singing]* No shoulder to cry on
No shoulder to cry on
No shoulder to cry on
No shoulder to cry on
No shoulder to cry on
No shoulder to cry on

Residents   Can't cry on your shoulder
When that shoulder's your own

Outside there'll be vultures who smell fear
when you moan
No shoulder to cry on
Can't cry on your shoulder
When that shoulder's your own
Outside there'll be vultures who smell fear
when you moan
The jungle will change your face
No shoulder to cry on
Can't cry on your shoulder
When that shoulder's your own
Outside there'll be vultures who smell fear
when you moan
You might be trapped here a while
But now is your time to smile
Cos when you leave this place the jungle will
change your face
O when I leave this place
O when I leave this place
No shoulder to cry on
No shoulder to cry on.

Singing Boy enters, head down, rushing past Tattoo Boy but stopping by Sharon.

Singing Boy   Alright? Have you heard anything about my bid?

Sharon   Not yet, no…

Singing Boy   Right thanks. *[Moving off]*

Sharon   Hold yer horses. Here yer are. *[Handing him an envelope]* It's your voucher for doing the interviews.

Singing Boy   Ah thank you…

Sharon   Told yer something would work out. You can use it at any shop.

Singing Boy   Can I use it in the Sainsbury's?

Sharon   No you can't actually… Hang on but there's the M&S, they got a food section ain't they… it's dear but still.

Singing Boy   Ah yeah, yeah. Thank you.

Singing Boy goes off.

Sharon   Aww. You know that voucher came just in time…he's had no money to buy food or anything and he was getting really down about it. *[Spotting another member of staff]* You going for a fag? I'll join you.

Interval.

Sharon and Singing Boy

Act 2

Scene 1 Breakfast club two

The beginning of a breakfast club, in the communal breakfast room.

Residents *coming in and out.*

Young Mum *is at the breakfast club with her baby.*

Young Mum	*[Asking interviewer]* Do you want tea?

Young Mum's Sister*, who is pregnant, arrives with a baby.*

Young Mum's Sister	Morning morning.
Young Mum	You alright babe? Do you want tea?
Young Mum's Sister	*[To interviewer]* You alright?

Ex-Resident *enters.*

Ex-Resident	Morning
Young Mum	He's into everything!
Ex-Resident	Not everything!
Young Mum	Good morning sir!
Ex-Resident	D'ya want a cup a tea or a glass of pee?! Cup of tea.
Young Mum	You want cereal? You want milk babe?

Tattoo Boy *enters.*

Ex-Resident *is feeding a baby.*

*[To **Tattoo Boy**]* You alright?

Tattoo Boy	I didn't sleep.

Towelling Robe *enters.*

Towelling Robe	Morning.

Bullet enters.

Bullet	Assalamu alaikum I don't eat the bacon! I'm a Muslim, I don't do the ham.
Young Mum	You should talk to him he's got bare stories man.
Young Mum's Sister	This guy yeah you need to get stories from *this guy*. Interview him.
Young Mum	Bare stories.
Ex-Resident	Yeah I used to work McDonald's and he used to ask me for one pound.

He started from the bottom, now he's here.

Bullet	*[Singing]* Started from the bottom, now he's here.
Ex-Resident	Apparently there's a ghost on the block.
Young Mum	But it's just the wind.
Ex-Resident	There's a spirit. It's like Casper.
Young Mum	Shut up it's the wind.
Ex-Resident	It's friendly.
Young Mum	Shut up man.
Ex-Resident	What's this place called?

All laughing.

Exactly: Raven Tower!

The interviewer tries to get the interview started.

I told you I don't live here now… I used to live here.

You still want to interview me. Him too, he's

got plenty stories.

Young Mum | Yeah, he's got bare stories.

Bullet | Now? Nah man…

Young Mum | Come you get a Westfield voucher fam.

Ex-Resident | I was here a long time.

Bullet | Been here two years, two and half.

Ex-Resident | Well, going through the process again so I'm in a similar hostel, again.

*[Trying to quiet the other **Residents**]* **Hush man, interview a gwan.**

Young Mum | Don't give him that. He'll choke on the skin.

Young Mum's Sister | What who told you your baby can't chew?

Young Mum | He can chew but he can't eat apple. Listen I'm his mother.

Young Mum's Sister | If he choke, I'll slap you.

Ex-Resident | Hush man, interview gwan.

Young Mum | Sorry. Yeah, okay hush.

Ex-Resident *tries to get the **Residents** to be quiet.*

Ex-Resident *moves his chair closer to the interviewer.*

Ex-Resident | For me I had personal circumstances which, which um…impacted my other things like, I was losing my job at the time and then…so yeah that was my issue, but just for the record yeah, I've actually been nominated from my place where I live now, I will be having a flat very soon so things are looking up.

Bullet *joins him.*

Nananananaa, there's personal circumstances so like…

Bullet   I got to Target because— *[Gives **Ex-Resident** a look, unsure]*

Ex-Resident   Nah it's alright gwan…

Bullet   I got to Target cos once I got shot, yeah basically what happened was like yeah urhmm…

Ex-Resident   Watford innit.

Bullet   I came out remand, I got bailed to Watford yeah my bail to Watford was for like urhmm, how long was my bail for Watford for? I was bailed to Watford for like three months for longer. Cos they said to me I couldn't come South London cos they didn't know if I was going to get into trouble or anything like that. They tried to say they imprisoned me for my own safety.

Ex-Resident   *[Laughing]* Jokes.

Bullet   Yeah but I don't believe that cos that's not really true is it. Like you imprison someone for their own safety, like that don't make sense. You should have just send me to Watford in the first place innit… Yeah got shot on my birthday.

Sharon walks through.

Ex-Resident   Yo Sharon, you alright?

*Sharon greets and talks with the **Residents**.*

Ex-Resident follows her around.

Bullet   To be honest I'm not gonna lie, to be honest, she's been the best help that I've ever seen in Target because before I didn't…she was brilliant, you see when you live here you have your key worker and she's the manager, I don't even go to my key worker and I go to her.

Sharon leaves.

Ex-Resident What pulls me back here? Cos um, basically the people you meet here cos you know when you live there you socialise with everyone, you, it's like a family thing cos you get to know a lot of people and like…because like, you've lived here for so long it feels like you're, like you still…

Sharon said to us the door's always open to us ex-residents and stuff and that we can come in, any time, any help that we want, they still want to help us out so…

Young Mum *[In agreement]* Fam. Yeah!

Ex-Resident I didn't have anywhere to go so and they gave me a roof.

Me? Family?… Yeah…the lack of has been from a young age…so…that sort of, I've learned to solidify myself and be strong yeah and bringing myself up cos it's been…

Ex-Resident gets up from the table.

Bullet No Target don't feel nothing like #!?&#! home, are you crazy? I hate this place with a passion.

If I wanted to be in jail I would have done a crime to get sent to jail. Every day the security guards ask for your ID. Course I made friends but you don't understand there is associates as well. Basically at any moment we can still get into a physical contact meaning that you are not my friend.

Bullet joins Young Mum at the table.

Ex-Resident   I do need experience to get a job so I'm doing football coaching, like coaching the kids that are in the community, and that way they can have fun playing football instead of being on the road and you know, being unsupervised.

I think that's a focal point, for me, because… there's a lot of stigma attached to the youth… and the trouble in London…and that sort of I think it's about publicity and…cos it's not all true, if you see the positive stuff that the youth do…

I think everybody gets fed up with the way the country's run if I can be quite honest… I think we're breeding a new generation, we're not just gonna be subservient any more.

I can only really talk about the young people that I engage with…that's the young people of East London.

Bullet   I'm from Jamaica but this is where I grew up.

[Indicating Young Mum's baby] Nah she's not mine but yeah, yeah I got children, a daughter.

She's with her mum.

She'll be four soon. Three and a bit…

Ex-Resident   I've got two seven-year-olds.

They live with their mum.

I think…the only message that I'd wanna put across is that…you can get anything you want, yeah, you just have to work for it.

I'd say I'm empowered, yeah, and I empowered myself with education. My friends

– *[Indicating the room of **Residents**]* cos this is what, you know, put a rocket up my ass.

You gotta understand it's about knowing one's self, you gotta know yourself, who am I gonna rebel against? Who could I then go and fight? I'm having a battle with myself now I might as well look in the mirror and throw something at it so…deal with it innit.

Well, my plan, I wanna be a PE teacher so I have to go through the whole education and…

Um…fatherhood…ah… You see it's more than just being…being there buying nappies and stuff like that it's…it's a kinship innit, you got…ah…it's hard, it's hard to like put into words.

Bullet   Like my family is the biggest thing in my eyes. To look after I love them so much but I don't call them cos I love them so much. I know that don't make sense, I'm like do you know how hard it is to care for someone, yeah when you really care about people in your heart yeah to actually phone them all the time is actually a hard thing, it's actually a hard thing, I don't even get to see my daughter as much.

Yeah so like not seeing my daughter changes me as well, cos like I am sad when I see other kids. Like I gotta take my daughter's mum court and stuff like that but I want to do that when I got my permanent house…

Young Mum's Sister   You want sugar?

Bullet   Yes three please. How many sugars would you like? Two? One sugar.

So when I don't see my daughter a lot as well yeah it hurts me a lot when I see other people with their kids.

Security Guard enters.

Ex-Resident   My dad the last time I seen him was around the time when I left here…yeah cos that was like from non-contact for about ten years to contact to… No, not really, that's just because I know he's a idiot, it's like, I didn't know back then but now I'm a big adult and oh, hey how you doing, you're a idiot yeah…all of a sudden wanting to do stuff and then…didn't have time…me like it can't be sometime-ish and there's history there, there's a whole behind it that's deep, deep, you can't talk about it and not…

Talk about it later? If that's your way to get my number I'll write it down!

What you talking about you don't even know how old I am, how old do you think…okay.

I think the anger's also, remember I talk about this generation nah, I've got to a stage where there was three generations in one room, my granddad, my dad and myself and we all, I felt like a stranger to everyone, there was no, no wisdom being hand down.

Bullet sings the first two lines of Sooner or Later by Shakka.

Bullet joins the Residents at the table.

Nah, hate's too much of a big word… I think… it's unfortunate that he's kinda small-minded.

Because, I'm gonna say this as well, this is, this

is – *[Indicating the others]* right here you see this group this is one generation of Target.

Bullet and Ex-Resident sing Sooner or Later by Shakka, competing with each other.

Tattoo Boy barges in, smashes a lightbulb in a lamp.

Residents call out to him.

Bullet	Don't #!?&#! with me man.
Ex-Resident	Nah leave it fam. *[Gently ushers Tattoo Boy away]*
Bullet	Fool.
Ex-Resident	Cool man.
Bullet	I'm doing this thing here man.

Security Guard leaves, muttering to himself.

Tattoo Boy   You recording? Sorry I forgot about that man.

Tattoo Boy clears up the mess he's made.

Ex-Resident   I think…there is #!?&#!. Cos everywhere has #!?&#!, cos not every day's perfect you know what I mean.

The loss of a good friend, Daniel, that made me think you know, you gotta understand negative things and positive things, do that in the name of him.

Very big impact which is why his face is painted on the walls.

That's why sometimes you've got to cherish your life cos you don't know what will happen to you and sometimes, like, well I do think about it a lot, I've got, I've got his T-shirt, you know what I'm saying he plays football with me. I put on his T-shirt underneath my shirt, I feel like yeah, like, he was here – *[Turns to greet someone in the room]* yeah, and I feel like he's still there, three of us because we had each other.

Residents begin to leave.

Shall we finish showing you around?

Scene 2 Portugal

Jade enters with Portugal.

Jade beatboxes.

Asian Young Mum is seen on one of the other floors.

Portugal   Who likes Darren?

Jade   *[Beatboxes]* You do!

Portugal   You're gassed bruv, I don't like Darren.

Jade   *[Beatboxes]* Whatever – why were you staring at him then?

Portugal   Shut up. You like Darren. Dem kids will be peak bruv. You like dem guys, I don't like dem guys man.

I like…dark guys yeah…dark-skinned coloured guys, someone that's darker than me I don't know why, but I do, I don't like light-skinned, like light-skinned people, so um…

Jade   *[Beatboxes]* What? Oh ask her if I can stay.

Portugal   Can Jade stay? See.

Jade   *[Beatboxes]* No I don't.

Portugal Nah she don't wanna do an interview.

So we um, yeah we started dancing then we exchanged numbers after the club, the next day…umm…it was one of my friend's birthday so I went to his house and he came as well, he came to like pick me up to go somewhere else I think. And then, no, he came to the guy's house as well, we stayed there, also partied a bit, or we danced, and then um…and then we got in his car, well he was driving his mum's car at the time but yeah we got in his car and

Jade and Portugal

then um…he dropped everyone else home and then he pinged me asking if I would like to go home with him, I said, 'Yeah! No problem why not,' and we went…but nothing happened like I think we stayed friends for a whole month but we would spend a lot of time together… I would sleep in his bed…but nothing would happen… I would um…I, I met his mum aaan… but we stayed friends for like, and then on my actual birthday, he met my mum, I said, you know what, she's taking me out to eat…so I wanted him to come with me…my mum liked him, so she was asking me to stay with him, and I was like I don't like him just yet! But when I like him, eventually, it can happen, maybe you know. And then I think she asked him if he liked me so he said yeah…it was okay, it was alright, it was just a awkward moment but then again it was alright…

Then one day we came back my friend was like, 'Oh, kiss her…'

So, I was drunk because we had champagne there, we had some champagne so we drank, all of us drank all of us was drunk so he actually did kiss me so from there…I think we started like that.

Portugal sings We Found Love *by Rihanna featuring Calvin Harris.*

And then everything was okay…until a certain time that one of my friends told him something that she shouldn't and this caused problems in-between us. Since then, it's like, we argue quite a lot…and then we, if we break up it's for the meaningless points…like…for no reason and he umm…you know when someone keeps breaking up with you for no reason? And it's like someone's taking the #!?&#! out of you… someone's just using you because he knows I love him therefore he's just trying to take the #!?&#!. As in I wouldn't be with nobody else, or I wouldn't cheat on him… I wouldn't do something out of order.

But guys it's just different, guys #!?&#! up all the time, guys can just turn their back on you…go and do whatever, come back and like, even give you STIs. For, for whatever reason because they just think that they have the power to do so. My ex, my ex, my very first love, we was together for like…a year and six months…on and off…off and on…on and off…

He took the #!?&#!…like, he took the #!?&#!.

I say the #!?&#! cos I was very young.

He cheated on me…but it weren't just any chick he 'beat' the nastiest dirtiest skankiest chick the grimiest chick in the whole of #!?&#! east. He caught chlamydia and we had sex therefore I caught chlamydia, never had nothing like that before, dunno why the #!?&#! he done that for just done it for like for no reason. The dirtiest, grimiest, skankiest, nastiest chick in the whole of #!?&#! east.

Yeah I know, so when I went to check up, I still forgave him…

Jade leaves.

…believe that…er…I took my medicine and

whatnot though at them times I didn't know the prosecutions of it like I didn't know how dangerous it was…and then…this boyfriend of mine now…he gave it to me twice already… from the time that…we broke up…and me stupidly, instead of me like…doing a check-up before…like before we get together, I just had sex with him. Cos he's my boyfriend so I don't think anything like, 'Oh, he's messing about.' Or he's going to be careful and is going to do it with condoms but he didn't. So he gave it to me…that was the first time, then the second time he gave it to me I fell pregnant…I fell pregnant and I had a miscarriage. For him… yeah…the chlamydia gave me some sort of fluid and the fluid kind of stopped it, stopped the pregnancy.

Portugal conjures up her Boyfriend. He approaches her as if to kiss her but then breaks away suddenly.

Portugal and her Boyfriend sing We Found Love by Rihanna featuring Calvin Harris.

Asian Young Mum above.

Yeah. At the moment we're not talking it's been almost…mmm yeah…his mum was really nice…his mum is a very lovely person. But I think since we've broken up she hasn't really… been bothered to speak to me and like… since we broke up cos one time we broke up for a very long time we broke up for like five months. So I think that I never really called her any more because end of the day she didn't seem that interested in talking to me so I never called her but then again, I do like her…like… she was a mother to me and whilst my mum couldn't be arsed my mum's never been here – she's never been to my house – *[Breathes]* his mum hasn't been here as well but at least she asks of me...she – *[Cries]* sorry...asks how I am, she tried to see if I'm alright but this was, she hasn't done it lately but hopefully, one day I'll call her and speak to her and see how she is, maybe she'll tell me why she sounds so upset with me but I reckon it's cos I never called her.

Sharon enters.

Sharon   *[Catching her finger on a hot tray]* Oh #!?&#!. Oh this? This is for the barbecue you're coming aren't ya? You're gonna come? It's to mark Daniel's...passing and that. I've been here cooking since five a.m., them lot are just sitting there, no you're alright, they're done now. I'll tell you what I can't wait to have two weeks off.

Scene 3 Daniel's wall

Young Mum   This is one of our laundry rooms.

No, it's usually quite quiet in the corridors. It's mostly in people's flats no one really jams the corridors.

Ex-Resident   Once in a blue moon.

Young Mum   No. No one jams in the corridors, I never seen anyone jam in the corridors.

Ex-Resident   She's a mother, she ain't got time to see but as far as I know, like.

Young Mum   We don't jam in the corridors, we go to each other's flats and stuff. Yeah, that's it, not really jam in the corridors, it's weird, it's like, I never thought of that.

Asian Young Mum	Um…I feel safe due to the cameras and security to a certain extent…but…sometimes I do get a bit freaked out because, obviously, they have their parties or you hear a lot of shouting a screaming, and, you know, when you hear arguments and fights so it does scare you and you don't know whether to go out and say something…or…or not, just in case if you do go and say something it does cause more of a problem for yourself, so, rather just not say anything.
Young Mum	When I first came here obviously, my sister upstairs, my other sister she was pregnant at the time—
Ex-Resident	Yeah they're bumping the system. *[Laughing]*
Young Mum	Shut up! My two sisters were here so I was lucky…my other sister lived next door to him, you can't not know him in the block to be honest and um…that's true there's not a lot of people that don't know you apart from if they're new.
Ex-Resident	I'm an entertainer.
Asian Young Mum	Best, rather keep myself to myself; yeah I see people, I talk to them, but it's not, I wouldn't like, go out with anyone cos you never know what could happen with anyone and I get scared of that…
	I don't want her growing up in a hostel, no way, it's not the way I was brought up, you know I have a family and it's just wrong… and personally my issue with hostel especially with this hostel is cos, because everyone's really young, there's a lot of drinks and drugs around, you know, I don't like having to take,

especially, having to go up, there's a lot of drug abuse where you can smell it in the lift and…

And she's most probably coming out buzzing out of the lift…

Seriously, that's not good it's not nice, and if I could smell it and if I could feel funny from it I'm sure she can so much more, she's so much smaller.

Young Mum Because they're new, cos they're new in the block but d'you know what yeah, I'm gonna be real with you, when I first moved here it was him, Tats and someone called Daniel, they were the three in this block, always together yeah, then tragically, Daniel got stabbed in Westfield I don't know if you lot heard about it yeah, he got stabbed in Westfield and I'm being honest to God, since Daniel died yeah, the block has just died down and Daniel always, every single morning, he'd walk past, you always saw him, in the reception, he was basically the nicest guy in the whole block…in the whole block, even if he didn't know you, he saw you in the lift, he'd say hi to you. Really cool guy, him and Tats and this crazy one, always everywhere together, ever since Daniel died it's like no one really comes to residents' meetings no more, no one jams really in the block…breakfast club was dead for like nearly a year, only started coming, livening up a bit… you don't realise the impact that one person has on the block until they're gone and that's what it was really.

Ex-Resident exits upset.

…and as you can see he's still upset about it he can't deal with it…even Tats, everywhere you know, he's I dunno if you saw him scribbling at breakfast club, he's very very artistic, yeah very about everywhere it's 'RIP Daniel, RIP Daniel, RIP Daniel' he's – shows how important he was in the block.

I should, um, show you the graffiti wall for Daniel yeah.

They move.

Ex-Resident *returns.*

Okay, can you let us in please? Cheers, come in, come in, come in, come in, this is our remembrance graffiti wall, whose idea was this? It was yours innit?

They are near the memorial.

Ex-Resident	He was just down to earth man, he was real.
Young Mum	Yeah. Remember our dear friend Daniel Johnson, to our love never to be forgotten, yeah.
Ex-Resident	Other people has passed away still…
Young Mum	It's not the same.
Ex-Resident	Yeah they hide things as well, a lot of things they hide but…as I say, wherever you are is, it's got its good and bad.
Young Mum	Like, no they just hide things cos…the way he actually died in Westfield, when we was putting the flowers and that, they put it outside, which I was angry about cos that's not where he last fell.

Ex-Resident Yeah! Where he fell was inside.

Young Mum They didn't wanna tarnish the image of Westfield yeah it's like okay, fair enough, you're a big establishment, but we've got a right as well you know?

The tour continues.

Sometimes it smells like wee, this is the nicest I've smelt lately – *[Turns attention]* we're doing a tour…this is one of our lovely residents.

*A **Resident** walks past.*

Opens door. We go outside.

***Garden Boy** is with a shovel, surveying the plants.*

Sometimes me and my sisters chill out here in the summer. We were supposed to have a barbecue here but they said for health and safety reasons we can't. Yeah, that's the bench for Daniel, come let's go in, it's a bit chilly. Apart from that, all the rest of the flats are the same, if you wanna go downstairs, I'll show you my mother-and-baby flat… Where's my keys?

Scene 4 Garden Boy

***Garden Boy** is outside.*

Garden Boy Nah. My mum has shown no interest in coming to see where I live or anything. My little brother…I see him, I see him as much as I can, as much as I can. He's nine this year, it's actually quite scary how quickly he's grown.

My dad? No, I didn't funnily enough. *[Laughs]*

I've met him once in my life when I was seventeen, he wants me to go up and see him, just obviously living here, I haven't got the money to buy a ticket to go to Birmingham.

But every day I apply for something in Tesco's, anything, I just don't wanna clean someone else's toilet and work in a McDonald's or anything like that, anything else I'll do, road sweeper, anything. Just couldn't clean a toilet. Gotta clean your own one innit, that's bad enough right! *[Laughs]*

A garden. I would love a garden. Cos of the anxiety disorder I told you about.

Basically I'd love to just go outside, breather, walk around the path, go back in. Or a balcony at least, just somewhere I can go outside, that's all I want.

Song: *Waiting for a Change*

[Singing] I hear voices in my sleep
And they say now's the time to leave
But I can't fight against gravity
So I'm just waiting for a change
There's an exit I could make
Of little white pills and scarlet razor blades
But that's a door I'm never gonna take
I'm just waiting for a change
One day
I'll be with my brother
And we'll live
A life like any other
Just not today
Just not today
So I'm waiting for a change.

No, I wouldn't, I love East London too much, I just love it here...just like the culture, obviously being cockney and all that, it's just...family.

...What David Cameron's like basically just put a leash around Stratford so, it's just getting really tight and all the money's getting hard there's hardly any schools around here any more.

Garden Boy

Yeah I don't know, I just don't think the Olympics should've been here, so they put the Olympics here and it just sort of um…cos like, I can put it like this, basically, I used to go to a shop, get a can of coke for 40p as soon as the Olympics come eighty pence, that's doub— even though it's only 80p it's still double the money – everything is just ridiculous, cos Westfield's got put everything's gone up in price, everything's too expensive you can't afford to live here any more and East London was originally built for the poor…

I love all the different like, um, like all the races all the different religions, it just, just makes me sorta happy that so many people can mix, so they moan about world peace but…everyone gets on perfectly fine don't they really?

I've never given up. Not once. I've never lost my self-pride. When I was on the streets, I would not quit and it got me places it got me here. I know I can definitely get my own place one hundred per cent but getting the garden and stuff…is like…a one in a hundred sort of thing but my adviser said I could probably, definitely get a balcony, if I live in a flat, fifth floor, no higher, balcony.

Jade and *Portugal* enter and sit on the garden bench, gossiping.

I really can't stress how much I don't want my little brother at my mum's. I brought him back here one night.

Yeah I know it sounds silly but my ambition is to just make sure my brother has the best possible life he can. That's my goal. *[Laughs]* That's my goal in life, millions, brother.

[Singing] I could leave this place right now
Sleep in doorways, let the flame go out
But I know there's something this is about
So I'm just waiting for a change
One day
I'll be with my brother
And we'll live
A life like any other
Just not today.

You're welcome – *[Laughs]* it's not much of a story…

Garden Boy exits.

Scene 5 Tattoos and piercings

Jade and Portugal are chatting with the interviewer. As ever, Jade speaks in beatbox.

Jade shows Portugal her tongue piercing.

Portugal	And I've got my tongue, my tongue I got it this year, February…my lip I got it 2009, October 2009, my nose I got it this year, October…
Jade	*[Beatboxes]* What about tattoos?
Portugal	Nah, I like piercings more than tattoos, I've got only one tattoo – *[Indicating her wrist]* It's my mum's name—

Jade beatboxes, indicates disapproval that Portugal has a tattoo of her mum's name.

She's my mum you know. Even though we don't get along… I've only got one. So, er, I did it. Yeah.

No, no I've always wanted her name because end of the day, I've only got one…she gave birth to me no matter what she did to me…I can still forgive her…but I wouldn't forget what she did. And even though she left me. *[To the interviewer]* I was um…seven at the time when she left. And then she went to Spain, she said she went to work but by the time I saw her again…seven years after…I see her with another baby! But, yeah. That's just how I see it…she's my mum and I have to like, accept it…

My dad?

Jade beatboxes, laughs at this.

I haven't seen him for years. Sometimes he tries contacting me on Facebook…trying to tell me some #!?&#!. Whatever.

Tattoo Boy is crossing the courtyard. Loud music starts up in one of the high-up flats.

Tattoo Boy   *[Shouting up at the window from where the music is coming]* Turn that #!?&#! off. Shut the #!?&#! up. *[Picks up a pebble from the ground and launches it at the window and walks off]*

Portugal   I haven't seen him for years. Sometimes he tries contacting me on Facebook…trying to tell me some #!?&#!. Whatever. If I have kids, yeah, I have to make them proud. My mum, I don't think my mum finished school so I want to finish it you know. I will be the first one to finish and I will… Even if I have to prove her wrong…I have to make her proud as well.

That you know what, even though…we don't have that sort of relationship…she still made it – *[Clears her throat]* because there's a lot of people in my family that think I won't make it because I am the way I am like, I go out a lot, I'm very outgoing, I like my friends a lot it's like I don't pay attention to my education… that's what they think. But I will make it. I know definitely I'll go university I'll do it. And I'll bring a degree back home and I'll show it to her and then I'll tell, I'll make her call my dad and tell him as well.

Jade looking at Portugal's tattoo once more.

Yeah. I call her her name I call her by her name I don't say Mum.

Where do you need to go? Oh you can cut through there – oh, you haven't got a fob…

Jade offers to take interviewer to the common room.

Scene 6 Cancelled breakfast club

Young Resident	Alright man?
Key Worker	I worked with kids and plus I've actually done a lot of work with the police, representation of young people.
Young Resident	Where's all the food man?
Key Worker	Nah breakfast club's been cancelled today…
Young Resident	What I'm starving…
Key Worker	There's some tea and coffee stuff left over…

I think my own, my own experience, so they call it experiential learning, yeah? Now, the emotional significant events that happened in my life, now I can use that in a positive way…and in the various jobs that I've been in, I've been fortunate where, I've had mentoring, I've worked with various people and establishments now, I think it's a case of, you gotta pass the baton, just that moment that you take to spend and talk with them, will change their lives.

Eritrean Girl Sorry. Where can I get a mouse? This one isn't working…

Key Worker Front desk, front desk yeah, you know security yeah… I think the first thing is just to listen. And then it's just to show them that you're human. And I think if you, if you work in a mechanical way: A, B, C, D, E… I don't find that works, I think you gotta be a bit more organical where you listen to what they're saying, listen to what they're doing and you just gotta mix it up with them, you know, have a conversation with them and show that you're in tune to what they're going through, so now if they're having a problem, and I don't have an understanding of what they're going through…how can I help them? Still hungry?

Young Resident Yeah man. They're ain't nothing in there.

Key Worker Get something from the shops innit?

Young Resident Bills to pay, bills to pay…money not come tru yet innit.

Young Resident exits.

Key Worker	Need. Need, need. Pain and isolation, that's the common ground, yeah. You got two hundred and ten people in here, now what about the people who are outside who haven't had this opportunity, what happens to them? Does it mean you have to…go down that dark and stormy road by getting yourself in trouble? To get help. Because who's gonna listen to you? Cos someone tells you no too many times, you're gonna just think, 'Sod it I've had enough', but sometimes you just need a chance and the one common denominator with the kids in here – all got a chance. Now they got one, it's just a case of what they do with it, and they gotta remember this is not their home. Any time I sit down with them, I tell them, this is not your home, you're only here for a moment, it's what you do with it.
Another Resident	Is breakfast club finished?
Key Worker	Not on today…cancelled. Okay…um…okay, I used to be a footballer and um, I was injured when I was younger and it was the police, police stop and search and um…so I was injured by police and…I had just signed a contract with Arsenal…and I played one game for England Under-21…so…and my shoulder was, it wasn't broken but all the fibres and the tissues were ripped in my shoulder…and I was playing cricket for Hampshire.
	…and then for me it was a case of, went to hospital that night, came back out and when I went home…to explain what had happened… family didn't really wanna know because as far as they were concerned, you're not supposed to get in trouble with the police—

Key Worker gets up.

It was looked upon as if, as if you bring shame on the family…so they were concerned more about, the shame on the family as opposed to what had happened so they didn't actually listen to the fact that I didn't actually do anything, the police were wrong and this is what they do…and because I took them to court, I had to take them so far to prove my point…to prove that they were wrong… and when I won the case every…nobody had nothing to say, except by that time I'd become more independent, I'd left home… and I'd gone to live in America for…after that happened, I didn't wanna be in England, didn't wanna be around anybody in this country, I left and lived in America for two years.

Bullet enters.

Key Worker and Bullet

Song: *Eyes Closed*
[Singing] Don't pack my bags I'll be fine on my own
Don't call the Feds, I've got my own phone
Don't need the dough, I'll work for it instead
This wound's way too big for this plaster
I'm slow but I'm learning to get faster
Time has healed me, but look at what's come after
I'll keep my eyes closed as I walk forward
If I can't see you, you can't slow me down
I'll keep my eyes closed as I walk forward
And touch the sky before I hit the ground
Can't you see my wings
Can't you see my wings
Can't you see my wings
Can't you see my wings.

Tattoo Boy enters and starts doodling on his arm with a biro.

Key Worker   I wouldn't say abandoned, I would say let down. And…as far as I was concerned, I knew from that moment, I'd never rely on anybody else again apart from myself. It made me stronger…but for some people it could've isolated them.

Key Worker and Bullet   *[Singing]* If you could see my eyes, you'd believe me
If I pronounced my I-N-G's you'd agree with every word I say
Don't friggin' patronise, I ain't one o them
I swear I'll show you every day of my life that I'm different

Key Worker   *[Singing]* No it ain't MY fault that I was born over here
But MY startin' point don't mean I won't get there
So show ME the cliff and I'LL show you no fear
I'll keep my eyes closed as I walk forward
If I can't see you, you can't slow me down
Can't you see my wings
Can't you see my wings
Can't you see my wings
Can't you see my wings.

Tattoo Boy   We're not talking to him, he's leaving. He's a traitor. He's gone Friday, won't even make it to Daniel's thing.

Key Worker   *[Laughing]* Yeah I'm leaving on Friday I just wanted a challenge, and plus it was managerial…it will shock a lot of them, because…the standard of work I work with, I don't mess around. Don't come to my support sessions if you ain't prepared, if you need help, ask, don't bury your head in the sand. You shouldn't put your life on hold for anybody, you're supposed to be going for it here, you're not supposed to be holding back…that's a good thing, dreams are a good thing, it's that transition, they gotta see that transition of what life really is.

*Sharon enters, indicating she needs to talk with **Key Worker**.*

*They exit with **Bullet**, leaving **Tattoo Boy** in the room.*

Scene 7 Playing with fire

Tattoo Boy

No I had a sister and er…like when I was younger and that, like primary school time, my mum was never really about, it was just my sister, my sister is more like my mum you know, my sister used to look after me more, take me out, dress me, feed me, everything.

Yeah I didn't even really see my mum until I started secondary school really, and that was it.

My life wasn't hard, it weren't harsh but it wasn't the best either you know what I mean? It could have been a lot more better I could have had a bit more probably a bit more love… and all that…but you know what it mean it swings both ways, I had to be good, to her for her to be good to me and that you know what I mean? Just didn't work out and then, I didn't mix with the wrong people cos I'm, they're my friends they're the right people they're not like they're rapists or anything not that they mug old grannies either…but it's just that we don't really stick to the rules, if you've got to make money you've got to make money.

Well really ever since I was young even before I started secondary school when I was in primary school…that cos where I used to live there was loads of factories and that…you know what I mean…and er…airport stuff and all that, so.

Silvertown… Like London City Airport there was all like their warehouses around there so even when we was young we could always break into the factories, like, at first it was just like a little fun thing to us, we thought the factory it was proper secured up but we didn't even realise we was bypassing it and that getting through it and that and it was um, a magazine factory, but we just used to rob it to get the football stickers and that, then we realised they was making sweets and there was a vodka, not vodka, like alcohol factory next door and that was nicking all the brandies and alcohol and we'd give it to our parents…sweet factories next to that, a French Connection factory there.

Yeah there was loads, we just… Yeah, it's a buzz as well obviously, you're getting chased and that and…

Yeah, even like looking back at it now, if I could go back to them times now and have the knowledge that I know now…I reckon I would be a #!?&#! multimillionaire; I wouldn't be in this situation right about now.

Tattoo Boy sings Playing With Fire *by Plan B featuring Labrinth.*

Yeah, even like looking back at it now, if I could go back to them times now and have the knowledge that I know now… I reckon I would be a #!?&#! multimillionaire; I wouldn't be in this situation right about now.

Scene 8 Memorial barbecue

At the barbecue marking the anniversary of Daniel's death. **Residents** *are eating and chatting.*

Young Mum I wouldn't want a big house, I would want something very normal, very…very calm, like inside my house, a very calm environment. Just about one or two bedrooms or however many kids I have…a nice living room and nice kitchen, something very cosy. I don't…I don't want something that's too much I don't like it cos I've never had too much therefore I wouldn't know how to deal with too much. So yeah.

Security Guard is patrolling.

Security Guard An ideal home? Hmmm…

Bullet is by the front entrance.

Bullet I think I'd probably have two houses, like a townhouse in Miami somewhere, one of those condos for when I'm working and that and then I'd have, like a quiet place…there's a lot of places I like in this world…has to be somewhere hot, tropical, with a nice view… probably Cuba, something sophisticated like.

Enter Eritrean Girl.

Eritrean Girl Is clean. And…mmm…nice…everything is, everything is clean, I'm happy anywhere.

Tattoo Boy Yeah I'd have a big house here yeah, I love London it's where I'm from. I'd definitely have a big house in London somewhere that I mean like, I'm thinking about some dream house you know what I mean… I don't mean Beverly Hills, I mean like the big house on top of the big hill and that, somewhere like, I don't know, I could probably make my own island like, what's his name, that Virgin geezer Richard Branson.

Sharon enters her office and sits at her desk.

Sharon My dream home…erm…it would probably be… erm…you know what I wouldn't even want a big, fancy place, just somewhere where there would be room for my daughters and their families, you know, good friends if they wanted to stay…erm…and just somewhere that, you know I enjoy being and feel safe you know…

The Priest I've been asked to come here today and share a few words about Daniel. We gather together on the eve of the anniversary of our good friend Daniel's death. We are still grieving. We still miss him. We still love him. Be with us as we still face uncertainty with the court case still going on. May there be justice.

We pray for peace in our hearts and in our community.

We are all human beings loved and loving.

We pray for unity of purpose and heart.

Keep far from us all danger and the temptation to strike back in anger. Help us to learn to love even better.

Give us peace in our hearts and in our community.

Bind us together, Lord
bind us together with cords
that cannot be broken.
Bind us together, Lord,
Bind us together, Lord,
bind us together in love. Amen.

Singing Boy exits and looks visibly shaken and overwhelmed.

Singing Boy   No no I'm fine. It's just I got my keys… I got my own place. I can't believe… you must come. Let me just sort the place out and everything and then I'll cook for you I will invite you to my place…

Scene 9 What next?

*A **Pregnant Resident** is on stage.*

Sharon   For the last three years we've always, there's been rumours that they're gonna close Target down…but, you know, from my point of view there isn't anywhere else really, this building is full all the time, even when we got a void we can fill it back to back you know erm…so what are they gonna do with all these young people, there is no other accommodation out there, there's very little accommodation available for anybody let alone a young person erm…and you know, some of these people if this place wasn't here would be living on the street. I'll give you an example. A young Asian girl, who…erm…had to leave because the parents were trying to get her put through an arranged marriage, she fled domestic violence, she left the area and came here to escape all that you know, and that girl has got nothing, you know so, she hasn't got family now because they don't wanna know, and she's fled, she's very scared for them to even find out where she is because you know, she informed us they'd take her back to her country and, you know, that would be it.

The biggest issue is the deposit nowadays you know, nobody's got a deposit to put down you know? It's not easy for anybody to get council accommodation any more, it's just really not, you know, it's so outdated that view. Years ago you used to hear it all the time you know about young people getting pregnant just so as they get their council house. Now I see it all the time, these young people even when they are pregnant they don't get council housing like that, there is nothing available for them. They get a bond scheme, they are not going into council accommodation they're going into private accommodation and you know the council will pay the bond for them but they are not secure, they might have to move out in six months, that council accommodation is just a myth, for me personally you know, I see it. It just doesn't exist any more.

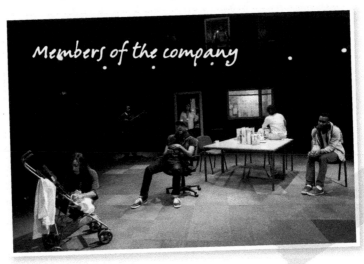

Members of the company

Sharon sings Stay With You by John Legend.

Who? Oh yeah Garden Boy. No he left…you won't believe it he smashed his room up. Yeah! The door was literally broken in half… No I think some of the residents had got hold of this 'legal weed'. Yeah they were selling it in the shop round the corner. We had four boys sectioned after smoking that stuff. Yeah! It was terrible. We had to call the police because it was getting ridiculous. But no, yeah he left. Yeah I can't, I'll email it later. Yeah, see you.

So what we going to do with you then?

End.

Epilogue

A cold January 2014. The Breakfast Room is empty. The building is unusually quiet.

Busker enters strumming his guitar in his worn winter coat and fingerless gloves. [Music Keys]

Security Guard	Keys O how I'm longing for those keys somewhere I can call my home my home call my home my home somewhere I can call my home my home call my home my home O how I'm longing for those keys

Singing Boy walks past looking distressed.

Singing Boy	No, no I'm fine. I just got my keys…I got my own place, I can't believe… you must come. Let me just sort the place out and everything and then I'll cook for you… I will invite you to my place.

*Exit **Singing Boy** as **Tattoo Boy** enters with paint splattered jeans.*

Tattoo Boy   I'm buzzing mate! I'm made up! It's nice man. I got my new curtains up the other day. I'm painting all the walls. Then everything's done apart from the floorboards. I'm gonna sand em, wax em, varnish em make it look proper decent.

*Exit **Tattoo Boy** as **Bullet** cycles on, hoodie up.*

Bullet   Yeah I've moved out of this place... but I ride my bike to Target every day to use the phone cause they're free.

Oh yeah, and to see Sharon.

*Enter **Portugal** with **Jade**, holding her newborn baby.*

Portugal   We've been moved Southend, Southend you know, but am with Jade and this little one so it's alright... and I'm gonna start my my first university course.

***Jade's** baby gurgles.*

*The girls exit as **Asian Young Mum** enters struggling with cases and baby.*

Asian Young Mum   We're getting evicted. They're evicting every mother and baby by the 20th of April. They could move us from London to Manchester, Birmingham, we just have to take whatever they offer by the deadline.

*Exit **Asian Young Mum** as **Security Guard** enters with his keys.*

Security Guard   Yeah I've been asked to leave, I've maybe two days left. I'm going to find it difficult to leave Target, work somewhere else, cause I know I'm gonna miss here so much.

*Exit **Security Guard** as **Sharon** enters holding a box of files.*

Sharon   Well, it's not a rumour anymore. They've cut support for anyone not seen as high risk, so they get a bed but nothing else. And um... I've been made redundant, yeah.

And, you heard about Thomas, you know, you met him in the garden didn't you? Some of the other residents found him...you know, it was awful...and he was doing really well.

But Thomas wasn't registered as high risk. That's the thing, they've cut support so you've got a young person who's fine one day and not the next...they're vulnerable, they're all high risk. I don't wanna be part that system... no way, no way.

Yeah. It's just a matter of time for this place.

She looks at her ID and takes it off, exits through door.

End.

Sharon

Activities

Young Mum and Ex-Resident

Explore the skills required for verbatim theatre

Home is a piece of **verbatim theatre**. It examines real-life situations and experiences, and quickly offers the audience specific points of view.

Verbatim theatre relies on the creative team to be accurate and respectful in the way that they use the material provided by real people. Working in groups of three, follow the steps below to explore the skills required for verbatim theatre.

Step 1

Person A: Tell a short story about something that has happened recently.

Person B: Listen carefully to the story that Person A tells. Try to focus on the exact words and phrases that they use.

Person C: As well as *listening* to the story, *watch* Person A carefully. Look for **gestures** and **mannerisms**, and listen carefully for **verbal tics**.

Step 2

Person B: Repeat the story back to Person A, trying as much as possible to use their exact words, phrases and order of events.

Step 3

Person C: Retell the story, repeating the physical gestures, mannerisms and any verbal tics that Person A used.

Step 4

Now repeat the task twice (using different stories), rotating the roles of Person A, Person B and Person C so that each person takes each role.

Key terms

verbatim theatre theatre that has been created using interviews, conversations, observations to form a script

verbatim the repetition of words in exactly the same way they were originally spoken

gesture a generally understood physical way of communicating a message

mannerism a distinctive habit or way of doing something

verbal tics sounds, words or phrases that are repeated during speech, such as 'um', 'er'

Step 5

a. What did you notice about how people told their original story? Think about how they spoke (tone, speed, hesitations, confidence, fluency, expressions, mannerisms and body language) and what they spoke about (an experience, personal belief, an emotional topic).

b. What made it easier or more difficult to repeat accurately what they had said? Think about how the story was structured, for example did it use repetition? Did it have a distinctive beginning, middle and end?

Activity 2

Compare oral and written stories

Key terms

monologue
an extended speech given by one character

script the written text of a play

a. Following on from Activity 1, each person writes down the story they told, as a **monologue**. Write it down quickly, without thinking or editing too much at this stage.

b. Still working in your groups, swap monologues and read each one aloud. Discuss:

   i. What has changed about the way in which each story has been told?

   ii. Do you think the stories have lost or gained interest for an audience?

   iii. Why do you think it might be more interesting for an audience to watch material that has been created in this way, rather than a traditionally crafted **script** that has been created by a playwright?

   iv. What are the challenges for an actor working with verbatim material, as opposed to reading words in a script that have been crafted and edited by a playwright?

Opening

Activity 3

Interpret stage directions

a. Reread the stage directions at the start of the play, 'An anonymous inner-city high rise…'. In groups, decide how you would stage the opening moments of the play. You may wish to do this in **tableaux** or as a more **naturalistic** presentation.

b. Consider the **atmosphere** that you wish to create for your audience. Think about:

- whether you want to create a tense atmosphere
- whether you want the audience to feel sorry for the interviewer who is approaching the housing block
- whether you want to make the audience comfortable or prepare them to confront some of their own opinions or experiences.

Act 1, Scene 1 Singing Boy

Activity 4

Explore the opening monologue

In this scene, Singing Boy talks about his reasons for being at Target. This monologue reveals information about his personality, his interests and his previous experiences.

a. Why do you think that the **creative team** chose to start the play with a long monologue and song?

b. Some critics may suggest that the first scene in a play needs to be fast paced and full of action. Why might this play be different?

tableaux a group of still figures representing a scene onstage

naturalistic a style of drama which aims to imitate real life closely

atmosphere the feeling or emotion that you wish to create for an audience

creative team is made up of key production members, including a director, set and costume designers, photographers and actors. It is the group of people that brings the playwright's ideas into being

c. In small groups, experiment with different ways of staging this monologue. For example, Singing Boy might be on stage by himself, or with other characters whom he interacts with. Are the lines delivered to the audience or other characters? Does he move around the stage?

Act 1, Scene 2 Breakfast club one

Activity 5

Write about 'home' and what makes one

In this scene, Tattoo Boy gives a definition of what he considers to be 'home' and the other residents give their own opinions.

a. In groups or pairs, discuss your ideas about what makes a home. Consider the objects and people that make a place home.

b. In no more than 50 words, write about what would make your ideal home, and why.

Act 1, Scene 3 Sharon's office

Activity 6

Improvise a scene between the senior manager and Sharon

Imagine that you are the senior manager of Target East and you are interviewing a new manager for the building. Complete the following in pairs:

a. Draw up a list of interview questions, taking into account what Sharon says about the qualities that a person might need to be a good social worker at a place like Target.

b. What answers do you think Sharon might give to those questions?

c. **Improvise** the interview between the manager and Sharon when she applies for the job at Target.

Act 1, Scene 4 New resident

Activity 7

Consider the emotions conveyed by beatbox

In the play, the character of Jade communicates only through the use of beatbox. When Nadia Fall originally talked to residents in the hostel, there were only a certain number of people to whom she could speak. Others were too shy or reluctant to come forward. Nadia decided to represent these 'untold stories' through Jade and her beatboxing.

a. In this scene, what emotions do you think Jade is experiencing? Include evidence from the text to support your points.

b. What effects do you think that the use of beatbox may have on the audience?

Key term

beatbox
the making of vocal percussion (often mimicking drum machines) using the mouth, lips, tongue and voice

improvise
create and perform a scene without detailed preparation or rehearsal

Act 1, Scene 5 The tour begins

Research the cost of living

In the play, Ex-Resident and Young Mum explain that some residents commit fraud by re-routing electricity and paying less than they should for it. For the residents of Target, every penny counts and throughout the play, several characters explain that they have very little money to pay for food.

a. Do some research to find out approximately how much it costs to:

    i.   rent a room or small flat in your area
    ii. pay council tax (for a year)
    iii. pay for water and electricity
    iv. buy basic food for a week.

b. What costs surprised you the most?

c. Talk to adult family and friends about what else they need money for, e.g. clothes, transport, phone and children.

d. How do you think some residents justify their theft from the electricity companies? Would you agree with their arguments? Explain why or why not.

Act 1, Scene 6 Dressing down

Act out a scene conveying conflict and the emotions of the characters

In this scene, Bullet is facing eviction because he has not been making the regular payments that he is supposed to make.

In pairs, stage this scene. Consider the following:

a. The scene takes place in an office. Are the characters sitting or standing? Does this change at any point? How can you use **posture** and **body language** to communicate the emotions and relationships of the two characters?

b. Bullet says very little during this scene. How can you use **facial expression** to communicate what he is thinking and feeling? What emotions do you think Bullet is experiencing? Is he scared of what is happening? Why does he say so little?

c. If you are playing the Key Worker, how can you use your **vocal skills** to communicate your character? Perhaps she or he is frustrated that attempts to help Bullet are not working. Perhaps she or he is angry that Bullet lies about not receiving letters from the housing association. Are there any moments where you might try and sound more sympathetic? Think about what Sharon says earlier in the play about the relationship between workers and residents at somewhere like Target. How can you communicate the difficulties that the situation presents?

d. At the end of the scene, the Key Worker realises that the interviewer is standing at the door. How might his or her body language and facial expression change once they realise a stranger has overheard the conversation?

Key terms

body language the way someone uses their body to communicate emotion, attitude and status

facial expression the way an actor uses their face to communicate

posture the way a person or actor stands

vocal skills methods used by actors to vary their voices to communicate aspects of character

Activity 10

Write a monologue exploring Bullet's motivation and attitude

a. Imagine that you are Bullet. Write a monologue to be performed straight after Scene 6, in which Bullet opens up about what has been happening and how he is feeling. Think about:

- the reasons he might give for his failure to pay
- why he lies to the Key Worker
- whether he is afraid of what might happen next.

b. Perform your monologue to your class, or group.

c. Compare the content of your monologue with one written by someone else.

    i. Are they different, or have you both communicated the same emotion or character? Why do you think this might be?

    ii. What information is there in the text that has informed what you have written, and the similarities/differences between your monologue and someone else's?

Act 1, Scene 7 Babies and boyfriends

Plan staging for contrasting accounts

This scene is one of the most powerful and shocking in the play, where two young mothers share their very different experiences of motherhood. Imagine you are staging this scene. Plan how you will bring out the contrast between their experiences.

mood the emotion and intensity on stage, created by the actors in performance

a. First, reread the separate accounts and list key features for each mother, including:

- where their flats are
- how they met their child's father
- their past and present relationship with the father
- their feelings towards their child
- their feelings about themselves and their future.

blocking deciding where, when and how actors move during a scene

b. Decide how to present the two accounts to bring out the differences between them. Consider the following aspects:

- **lighting**
- how to convey the sense of being 'trapped' in the top flat
- what props to use to convey the different **moods**
- what sounds to include as background
- **blocking**.

lighting the use of different lights to help the audience see the performers, and to create mood and setting

Note down the decisions that you make. For professional productions, a Stage Manager will create a Prompt Book which is a copy of the script with notes made on blocking, props, lighting changes and sound cues.

Act 1, Scene 8 Bullet

Activity 12

Write a news report about the shooting

Write a newspaper or TV report about the shooting that Bullet describes. Bullet provides some detail about what happened, but you will need to expand on it further. You may wish to include the following details:

- a headline
- the geographical location, time and date of the event
- a description of the gunman and whether he was on foot, on a motorbike or in a car
- information about whether the gunman has been caught
- the reason for the shooting
- quotations from witnesses and the victim (Bullet).

Act 1, Scene 12 This is England

Activity 13

Writing an alternative viewpoint

Some of the views expressed by Tattoo Boy in this scene are controversial. Being so honest about his opinions shows how much he trusts the interviewer. However, some of what he says could be considered inaccurate and offensive.

a. Discuss Tattoo Boy's statements about:

i. majorities and minorities
ii. the likely demography (population) in one hundred years' time
iii. what immigrants contribute to the economy and society
iv. whether English people live abroad and take their culture to other countries

v. shops that cater for particular nationalities

vi. his girlfriend's background.

b. Write a letter to Tattoo Boy, challenging some of his statements and putting forward a different viewpoint. Even if you agree with some of his ideas, try to take a wider perspective on the issues he raises – all of them are complex and need careful thought.

c. How can we help people to take a more informed and open-minded approach to the world around them? Come up with three suggestions for promoting tolerance, education and understanding among young people.

Activity 14

Plan how to present contrasting characters

Tattoo Boy and Singing Boy both appear in Scene 12, but they are contrasting characters so they need to be presented very differently.

a. How might you use facial expression, vocal skills and body language to communicate differences between the two boys to the audience?

b. How would you use the space to show their different personalities? For example, Tattoo Boy is very vocal, and might move around a lot, whereas Singing Boy is shy and may not wish to draw attention to himself.

c. The stage direction tells us *Singing Boy enters, head down, rushing past Tattoo Boy but stopping by Sharon*. What does this tell us about his feelings and personality?

Explore different viewpoints through forum theatre

forum theatre
theatre which
allows people
to participate
and explore
different points
of view. See
the work of
Augusto Boal

Forum theatre is a way of exploring different points of view. Follow the steps below to explore the issue of rising crime in the area in and around the Target hostel.

Step 1

The class should divide into four groups:

1. Residents of Target

2. Case workers and managers at Target

3. The police

4. Residents of private homes near the Target hostel

Imagine that these 'stakeholders' are attending a community meeting as a result of recent crimes, including the death of Daniel, who was stabbed at Westfield. Concerns have been raised about the safety of residents, including those who live near the hostel. The purpose of the meeting is to allow the different stakeholders to express their views and opinions, and to come up with ways of improving safety in the area and reducing the crime rate (including violence and the use/sale of drugs).

Step 2

Each group elects a representative, then discusses what he or she should say at this meeting, based on information from the play. What are the issues that are important to them? What resolutions might they suggest? What do they want the outcome of the meeting to be? For example, the residents who live near Target may want a greater police presence, or to impose a curfew on the residents of Target to try and reduce the amount of crime that happens at night.

Step 3

Choose a chairperson for the meeting. Each group's representative takes turns to present their ideas. As the meeting progresses, other people in the same group can volunteer to represent the group by shouting 'FREEZE!'. If this happens, the meeting halts whilst there is a changeover of representative.

Step 4

At the end of the meeting, the chairperson should:

   i. summarise the points made by each group
   ii. decide on measures that will be taken to improve safety and security for all of the stakeholders
   iii. agree to a number of activities to create a greater sense of community at Target, where people can sometimes feel lonely and isolated.

Activity 16

Write a diary entry in role as a character from the forum theatre exercise

After completing the forum theatre activity, write a diary entry for your character reflecting on the meeting. Consider:

- what went well
- what were the more controversial comments or ideas that people suggested
- whether your character got the outcome they wanted
- what needs to happen next to make sure that the safety situation improves.

Act 2, Scene 1 Breakfast club two

Activity 17

Write a poem or song lyrics to express a character's thoughts

In Scene 1, Bullet performs part of a song. Choose one of the other characters in the play, and write a short poem, rap or song lyrics to summarise their experience of being homeless or living in a hostel. Try to include details from the play which explain their worries, hopes and dreams.

Act 2, Scene 3 Daniel's wall

Activity 18

Improvise a scene involving Daniel

Daniel is a character that we never meet because he has been killed, but he still has a big influence on the other residents.

a. Read through Scene 3 and note down what we find out about Daniel.

b. Improvise a scene where Daniel is present, e.g. in a residents' meeting or the breakfast club. Think carefully how to present aspects of Daniel's character in this performance.

Act 2, Scene 7 Playing with fire

Activity 19

Explain the link between scene title and content

Why do you think this scene is entitled 'Playing With Fire'? Write your answer in at least two paragraphs, using quotations from the play to explain your reasoning.

Act 2, Scene 9 What next?

Write a persuasive letter arguing for funding for Target

Read Sharon's monologue in Scene 9. Write a persuasive letter to the British government's Housing Minister, persuading him/her to increase funding so that places like Target can continue their vital work with young and vulnerable people.

Remember to use persuasive devices such as:

- **rhetorical questions**
- exaggeration and emotive language
- **imperatives**
- fact and opinion
- repetition
- statistics
- **tricolon** (rule of three).

Your letter should be written in **Standard English**, and be laid out in a conventional way, with an appropriate formal greeting and ending.

Key terms

rhetorical question a question used for effect, which challenges the reader/listener to consider something, without expecting a reply

imperative a form of verb that gives instruction or a command

tricolon (rule of three) a rhetorical device that uses a series of three parallel words, phrases or clauses, e.g. I came, I saw, I conquered

Standard English the form of English language widely accepted as the usual correct form

Epilogue

Key terms

epilogue a short addition at the end of a play to conclude or comment on what has gone before

thrust configuration a performance space where the audience are seated on three sides

levels the use of different heights which can help create a sense of status or location

Activity 21

Respond to the epilogue

Remind yourself of the **epilogue**. What do you think it adds to the play as a whole and what do you learn from it?

Activity 22

Design a set for *Home*

The interviewer is taken through a variety of different areas at Target, the fictional hostel in the play. In the original National Theatre production, a basic **thrust configuration** was used, which allowed the audience to gain different perspectives depending on where they were sitting in the theatre. Different **levels** were used to create a sense of the multistorey building in which Target is located.

a. After reading the play, note down the different locations through which the interviewer is taken.

b. Then, in pairs or small groups, decide how you would design a set for the play. You should keep it basic so that it requires minimal scene changes, but allows the actors to create a sense of different rooms and external, as well as internal, locations. For example, you may wish to use a series of flowerpots to suggest the garden, or different styles of chairs for different rooms. You could use a chair on wheels to suggest an office, whereas a plastic chair might suggest a communal space. Think, too, about how props such as boxes of cereal could suggest the breakfast club.

c. Consider how you could use lighting to alter the size, shape and atmosphere of a room or performance space. For example, you could use a small, focused patch of dim light to represent a small room, whereas you might like to flood the stage with bright light to suggest the outdoors. You could also use practical lights to represent different interior spaces. For example, you might use fluorescent strip lighting to suggest a communal area or an angle poise lamp to suggest an office.

d. Present your ideas as a series of sketches or a storyboard, or simply describe what you would use for each scene.

Activity 23

Develop skills for multi-roling

In the original performances of *Home*, each actor played at least two characters. Choose your two favourite characters in the play (they must appear in different scenes to each other) and two scenes in which they appear. Focusing on your use of facial expression, vocal skills and body language, rehearse and perform these scenes in small groups, showing as much differentiation between the characters as possible.

Ask your group for feedback on what they felt was strong about your performance and areas that you could improve. From this feedback, set yourself a target to develop one aspect of your drama skills.

Activity 24

Plan a playlist as background music for the production

Nadia Fall, who wrote and directed the National Theatre's production of *Home*, considers music to be an essential part of the play. Music is important in most people's lives, but particularly in the life of a young person.

Create an alternative playlist that you think would be a successful soundtrack to the play and justify your choices.

Activity 25

Create verbatim drama

Verbatim is often used to highlight particular issues or problems within a local community. Using ideas you have developed from studying *Home*, create a 10-minute verbatim drama based on a theme or issue that is important to you and the people around you.

Themes you might consider are:

- school life
- bullying
- friendships and relationships
- family
- unemployment
- the future
- money
- a local or national political issue.

Work through the stages below.

1. **Interviews:** You must tell people that they are being recorded, and why. You should offer them the opportunity to be part of the editing process, and ensure that you remove any parts of the interview that the speaker is unhappy with.

2. **Research:** The type of research that you undertake depends on your subject matter. It could include further information about a real-life event, a real person, or the location in which the scene(s) take place. You may choose to use real news footage, songs or radio excerpts in your performance so this might also form part of your research.

3. **Editing:** What specific elements of a character or situation do you wish to emphasize? How much time on stage does this character have? Is there anything the real-life character wishes you to remove?

4. **Rehearsal:** Providing your actor with the edited recordings of interviews will help them to create an accurate and respectful rendition of their character. Consider blocking carefully, and take into account the set design that you have chosen to use.

5. **Performance:** Some verbatim directors ask their actors to wear earphones whilst performing so that they can hear the original speeches. Other directors rehearse the actors in such a way that this is not necessary. When performing, remember to address and look at the audience as if they are the interviewer – this is one of the common conventions of verbatim theatre and creates a strong actor-audience relationship.

If you are interested in learning more about verbatim theatre, you could research the work of Alecky Blythe, Nicholas Kent, David Hare, Gillian Slovo and Richard Norton-Taylor.

Making the play

Home rehearsal

Home was first performed in The Shed, a temporary studio venue at the National Theatre, London, on 9 August 2013 (previews from 7 August). The original cast list below shows that as well as the actors on the stage, there are many other roles behind the scenes, which you will learn more about in this section.

Cast list

Young Mum/Portugal	Michaela Coel
The Priest	Jonathan Coote
Security Guard/Key Worker	Trevor Michael Georges
Singing Boy/Ex-Resident	Kadiff Kirwan
Sharon	Ashley McGuire
Jade/Towelling Robe	Grace Savage
Bullet	Shakka
Eritrean Girl/Asian Young Mum/ Young Mum's Sister	Antonia Thomas
Tattoo Boy/Garden Boy	Toby Wharton

Other parts played by members of the company

Director	Nadia Fall
Designer	Ruth Sutcliffe
Lighting Designer	Ciaran Bagnall
Movement Director	Jack Murphy
Music	Tom Green and Shakka
Music Director	Gareth Valentine
Fight Director	Kate Waters
Sound Designer	Mike Walker
Company Voice Work	Richard Ryder
Production Manager	Paul Handley
Staff Director/ Dramaturgical Support	Rob Drummer
Stage Manager	David Marsland
Deputy Stage Manager	Fiona Bardsley
Assistant Stage Manager	Cat Fiabane
Costume Supervisor	Lucy Walshaw
Props Supervisor	Rebecca Johnston
Assistant to the Lighting Designer	Kate Greaves
Project Draughting	Emma Morris
Casting	Charlotte Bevan
Production Photographer	Ellie Kurttz

Director, Nadia Fall, during rehearsals

I have worked with young people in countless participatory projects over the past fifteen years using drama, music, film and creative writing techniques to engage them, but most of all to trigger their imaginations and give them a voice. I found myself working with some very marginalised young people – in pupil referral units, homeless hostels and mental health settings across the country. What I noticed almost immediately was how quickly time would pass when working with young people and that I would feel exhausted, yet more invigorated, working with them than with any other groups. I also learned pretty quickly that my well-meaning, 'do-gooder' sentiments, of somehow going in and saving the forgotten

youth from the harsh world of hard knocks, was so off the mark. These young people were going through hardships and challenges that I could not begin to imagine, and what they didn't need from me was another teacher, social officer or, worse still, therapist. Please don't misunderstand me, these professions are invaluable and amongst them we find individuals who can save a young person in so many ways, but that was not my place.

Where there would be a meaningful meeting between us, would be as fellow artists, equals, learning from each other and making work together. Teachers would often be amazed – 'Oh he's usually trouble' – or psychiatric nurses – 'She never normally talks' – but there was nothing miraculous in what I was doing. I was just a stranger with no prior judgements. I wanted them to be free from scrutiny and safe in the few hours we had together to focus on our creative work.

My passion for working with young people was shared by my close university friend, Esta Orchard, who has been an avid campaigner for young people since we graduated. We were both keen to collaborate and somehow create a project which had both artistic merit and the potential for social change.

Jump-cut to the London riots of summer 2011 when, following the death of Mark Duggan, many young people took to the streets in London and beyond. The media and politicians were quick to portray these young people as feral creatures, wild and almost subhuman. I remember a distinctly bleak mood at the time from a public who wanted to understand but quickly lost patience, becoming fearful, with an ever-more cynical distrust of young people. It seemed that the gap between the already disenfranchised inner-city youth and everyone else had widened more than ever before. Esta and I, both as mothers and as practitioners, felt compelled to respond creatively and urgently.

It was at this time that Esta was writing an environmental psychology thesis and interviewing young people who had taken part in the riots. She was keen to use testimonials to gather data that could lead to research and even policy change. We both felt more and more eager to create a piece of theatre that gave young people a voice. We began to experiment when we were asked to contribute to a mental-health consultation, attended by policy makers. We used testimonials from young people and very simply staged them as talking heads, which had a powerful effect on the audience. That year I directed two verbatim plays, as a way of exploring the form, discovering the potential and analysing the transition from testimonial to live performance.

Verbatim script is made up of real life conversations and interviews, so the characters in *Home* are representations of real people and these are their own words.

About 20% of the material used to create *Home* was based on observations and did not come from directly recorded material. I do not adhere to material being repeated or spoken in absolutely the same way it was originally spoken. There needs to be room for manoeuvre for the actor, as long as we keep the intention and spirit of what is said. The endeavour is not to mimic.

Esta and I thought of many groups we both shared connections with through our respective work and we were both interested in rooting a narrative in a specific place, giving the stories of these young people a geographic anchor. Esta had links to a network of hostels, each of which houses vulnerable young people, who would otherwise be homeless, and so we decided to approach one of the largest in East London. I carried out interviews with the residents and some staff at the hostel between autumn 2012 and spring 2013, collecting over thirty hours of interviews that have formed this play. My only regret is that I was unable to include all of the stories, so generously shared with me.

I would like to thank everybody who took the time and had the courage to speak with me, there simply would be no play without you. I hope this play will give a voice to the all-too-often silenced young people of our capital, and may it go as far as to impact policy affecting tangible changes in the way provisions are made for vulnerable young people in the UK.

Nadia Fall

Interview with Grace Savage, cast member

Why were you interested in performing in *Home*?

I met with Nadia, the director. She was looking for a beatboxer and someone had recommended me. I connected with her instantly and was really inspired by her passion for the project. I also think any performer at the beginning of their career would be silly to turn down a role at the National Theatre!

Did you feel a particular sense of responsibility to the real people that you were representing on stage?

My character was the only one that wasn't based directly on a real person so I didn't feel the responsibility in the same way the other actors did. Initially I was employed to be a musician to help create the live soundtrack for the play. Then in rehearsals one day, Nadia stuffed a jumper up my top and told me to 'speak' in beatbox. My character then ended up as a young pregnant girl in the hostel, who represented all the other residents Nadia interviewed or saw, who weren't given a direct voice in the play. We did a closed showing specifically for the residents of the hostel and the people that the characters were based on. We were all incredibly nervous before that performance. We wanted to tell their story truthfully and do it justice … thankfully they loved it. The performance was raucous, raw and alive - they were walking across the stage to use the 'door' that was set up on stage, babies were crawling across the floor, people were, crying, laughing and shouting out when they recognised a particular character trait of theirs being played. It was a very emotional experience. We also did a Q+A afterwards with politicians and gave the young people the opportunity to question them about the housing and homelessness crisis for young people. It was the kind of experience that reminds you why we should be making theatre and art in the first place - to tell stories that truly connect with people and that have the potential to create real change in people's hearts and communities.

Why do you think it is important to tell stories like this on stage?

There are a couple of quotes which I think are very relevant to this question:

'You can't be what you can't see' – Marian Wright Edlemen

'If you want to make a human being into a monster, deny them at the cultural level any reflection of themselves' – Junot Diaz

In my opinion, art should never just be for the upper classes. Often, commercial theatre (especially big budget theatre) is *made* by privileged people, *performed* by privileged people and then *watched* by privileged people. How is that going to challenge anyone or change anything except reinforce the idea that only certain people are worthy of being represented? Having stories like *Home* on a stage like the National Theatre is extremely important – it gives value and meaning to the lives those who aren't usually represented in a positive light and it allows more privileged people to empathise with them and understand them.

You're a beatboxer and that was a large part of how you realised your character – could you tell us a little about that?

Once we'd made the decision for me to 'speak' in beatbox I would have the conversation with the person I was sharing the scene with in dialogue first, so that I could fix intentions to what I was communicating. Then I would replace that dialogue with improvised beatbox sounds. It seemed to work as audience members told me afterwards they felt like they knew 'exactly what I was saying' – which of course could have been entirely different for each of them. Audiences like to make the stories they are seeing on stage relate to them. In order to empathise with characters, you need to understand them and in order to understand them, you have to relate them to your own life – so when my character was annoyed about something, they could project their own feelings and emotions onto her. Because beatboxing is such a **guttural**-sounding thing, people had a really instinctive response to it.

Grace Savage in rehearsal

Key term
guttural harsh sounding, throaty speech

Context

'I've been here nearly two years…and it's been struggling, struggling living here, it's just hard.'
(Garden Boy, Act 1, Scene 5)

Home is set in one of the largest hostels in East London, which provides shelter for vulnerable young people who otherwise would have nowhere to go.

Centrepoint and Homeless Link are just two charities in the UK that provide housing and support to people who are homeless or at risk of homelessness. In particular they support young people and carry out research into youth homelessness. The facts and figures below have been provided by both of these charities.

Scale of youth homelessness

Centrepoint reports that each year more than 150,000 young people ask for help with housing because they are homeless or at risk of homelessness. A recent Homeless Link report stated that nearly half of people living in homeless accommodation services are aged between 16 and 24 and that without adequate support, homelessness can impact their education, employment prospects, health and wellbeing. It is also more likely to result in them being homeless when they are older. However, it also states that in spite of being homeless, as many of 65% young people are in education, studying, employed or on a training or apprenticeship scheme.

Leaving home

In *Home* we encounter a number of young people from different backgrounds who all have different reasons for why they are staying at Target East. Across the UK , more than two thirds (67%) of homeless young people ended up without a home because of a breakdown in their family relationship and over half, 58%, of homeless young people have encountered violence at home. Arguments occurred every single day in the homes of 59% of homeless young people and more than one in four (27%) homeless young people say that their family home was not a loving environment . More than half (53%) of homeless young people say they couldn't talk to their families about things that were bothering them while 7% of homeless young people cited their parent's not accepting their sexuality as a cause of family arguments, compared to 2% of the general population.

Rough sleeping

Homelessness for young people can mean that they stay at friends' houses or end up sleeping rough. They need appropriate emergency and longer term accommodation to help them avoid this but it can be hard for them to access affordable and suitable housing.

In 2016/17, 761 people under the age of 26 were seen rough sleeping in London – the number has more than doubled in the last six years.

- 47% of homeless young people who have slept rough have been victims of assault or physical abuse

- 19% of homeless young people have been victims of sexual abuse

- 52% of homeless young people who sleep rough do so for 2–7 nights

Desperate measures

- 26% of homeless young people have stayed with a stranger
- 12% have committed a crime to be taken into custody to avoid freezing to death
- 9% have attempted to admit themselves in to A&E.

(All statistics from Centrepoint)

More information about both charities can be found on their websites:
- The Centrepoint Helpline is for any young person aged 16-25 who is worried about homelessness. The number is: 0808 800 0661 / http://centrepoint.org.uk/
- Homeless Link https://www.homeless.org.uk/

Glossary

atmosphere the feeling or emotion that you wish to create for an audience

beatbox the making of vocal percussion (often mimicking drum machines) using the mouth, lips, tongue and voice

block/blocking decisions on where, when and how actors move during a scene

body language the way in which someone uses their body to communicate emotion, attitude and status. It can include posture, how they sit, eye contact and physical contact

configuration the way in which a stage or performance area is created

creative team is made up of key production members, including a director, set and costume designers, photographers and actors. It is the group of people that brings the playwright's ideas into being.

epilogue a short addition at the end of a play to conclude or comment on what has gone before

facial expression the way in which an actor uses their facial features to communicate emotion and attitude

forum theatre the way in which an actor uses their facial features to communicate emotion and attitude

gesture a generally understood physical way of communicating a message. For example, shaking hands can mean 'hello' or 'goodbye'

guttural harsh sounding, throaty speech

imperative a form of verb that gives an instruction or a command

improvise create and perform a scene without detailed preparation or rehearsal

levels the use of different heights, for example sitting, standing or using different height platforms/staging which can help create a sense of status or location

lighting the use of natural or electric light to allow an audience to see particular action, highlight and define different areas of the stage or conceal aspects of the stage during performance

mannerism a distinctive habit or way of doing something

monologue an extended speech given by one character

mood the emotion and intensity on stage, as created by the actors in performance

naturalistic a style of drama which aims to imitate real life closely

posture the way in which an actor stands to communicate age, fitness, attitude, or relationship to other people

rhetorical question a question used for effect, which challenges the reader/listener to consider something, without expecting a reply

script the written text of a play

Standard English the form of English language widely accepted as the usual correct form

tableaux a group of still figures representing a scene onstage

thrust configuration a performance space where the audience are seated on three sides

tricolon (rule of three) a rhetorical device that uses a series of three parallel words, phrases or clauses, e.g. I came, I saw, I conquered

verbal tics sounds, words or phrases that are repeated during speech, such as 'um', 'er', 'like', 'sort of', often used to give the speaker time to think

verbatim the repetition of words in exactly the same way in which they were originally spoken, i.e. 'word for word'

verbatim theatre theatre that has been created using interviews, conversations, observations and written material to form a script

vocal skills methods used by actors to vary their voices to communicate aspects of character. These can include pitch, pace, pause, projection, accent, dialect, volume and tone